GREAT GARAGES

Sheds & Outdoor Buildings

101 Projects You Can Build

Written by
Connie Brown

HOME PLANNERS, LLC
Wholly owned by Hanley-Wood, Inc.
3275 W. INA RD., SUITE 110, TUCSON, ARIZONA 85741

CONTENTS

Book Design:
Karen Leanio, Graphic Designer
Paul Fitzgerald, Senior Graphic Designer

Editor:
Paulette Mulvin, Senior Editor

Cover Photo:
©Peter Aaron/Esto
Cover Plan Designed by
    Jay C. Walter, AIA
    Entasis Architects, P.C.

Back Cover:
Digital Rendering by Shannon Graphics

Published by Home Planners, LLC
Wholly owned by Hanley-Wood, Inc.
3275 West Ina Road
Suite 110
Tucson, Arizona 85741

Distribution Center:
29333 Lorie Lane
Wixom, Michigan 48393

CEO and Publisher:
    Rickard D. Bailey
Director of Publishing:
    Cindy Coatsworth Lewis

Library of Congress
Catalogue Card Number: 96-077484

ISBN: 1-881955-33-8

10 9 8 7 6 5 4 3

First Printing September 1996

Printed in the United States of America.

On The Cover: Luxury plus in a
three-car garage! The second floor
of this plan, G302, is a full guest
suite or home office. See page 33
for more information.

BUILDING BASICS

For Garages, Sheds & Outdoor Buildings

A garage is the perfect complement to a comfortable home, serving as a shelter for precious vehicles, a storage space for tools and lawn equipment and often as a work space for the home mechanic. But sometimes you need more—more work space, more storage, or even just more amenities. The projects included in this book run the gamut from simple, utilitarian garages to facilities that accommodate three cars plus office space or even a complete guest apartment. In addition, there are plans for sheds, cabanas and pavilions, barns and stables, and lovely, breezy gazebos. Each is designed with you in mind and can be appointed to fit in perfectly with whatever style home you have. Best of all, complete construction blueprints are available for every plan.

Projects such as those in this book are very do-able! With an understanding of the basics, the right tools for the job, a set of our plans—plus an adequate supply of time and patience—you can create a useful and practical work area, or a charming and restful hideaway.

ADVANCE PLANNING

Project Selection

The first step, of course, is to decide on the project. Of all the possibilities, what does your home, your property, your family need the most: a two-car garage with office space, a whimsical gazebo, or a practical tool shed?

If you already know what outdoor structure you want to add to your property (a garage with a guest suite, for example) then move right along to the next easy step. Simply select the size and layout you prefer from over 20 plans with living space shown in this book. With all the possibilities fresh in your mind, take a slow walk around your property and decide which of the outdoor structures is the best match in form and function to your family's needs and the space and budget you have available. Then turn to page 92 for order information, and you're on your way.

You'll also need to consider if you have the time and expertise to build the project you've selected, or if you will need to involve a licensed contractor for all or part of the work. Once all that's decided, refer to page 92 to order the plans you need and turn your thoughts to site selection.

Site Selection

Site selection depends on a number of things: what you are building, its purpose, who is going to use it, its accessibility, its appeal, and any applicable building codes and setback.

Location: If you decide to build a garage, you will want to consider accessibility to the driveway and the house. You may even decide to connect the garage to the house via a breezeway. If your choice is a stable or barn, your first consideration will be for the animals to be housed there. You'll want enough room to allow for corrals as well as some comfortable distance from the house. If you are building a gazebo, it will likely become the focal point of your property and, as such, should occupy a prominent space.

Drainage: If your property has moist areas, avoid them if you can. This is particularly true for gazebos, sheds and other smaller structures. The alternative is to provide a dry, firm base by adding sand and gravel fill under the project to aid the drainage of the site.

Utilities: Plan ahead for any utilities your project may require: electricity or water for sheds, garages and guesthouses, or gas for heat or a grill. Call your local utilities providers for locations of underground cable and water lines, if necessary.

BUILDING BASICS

Building Permits

When your advance planning and site selection are complete, it's time to obtain the required building permits. Separate building permits are usually needed for each construction discipline: one for the structure, one for the electrical work, one for the plumbing, one for the heating, and so on. Specific requirements for each vary from region to region across the country. Check with your local building officials before you begin your project to determine which permits you need. If your project is small, permits may not be required.

Building Codes

Along with building permits come the codes which must be met. These codes are usually imposed by county or city governments. Codes are required to ensure that your project meets all standards for safety and construction methods. A local inspector will usually check the progress of your project at various stages, and there could be more than one inspector, depending on the utilities you incorporate.

> **Check with your local building officials before you begin your project to determine which permits you need.**

Some of the regulated items the inspectors will check include: distance of project from property lines, handrail heights, stair construction, connection methods, footing sizes and depths, material being used, plumbing, electrical and mechanical requirements and neighborhood zoning regulations.

Site Plan

Creating a site plan, or detailed layout of the project on the property, is important when incorporating a new addition to an existing landscape. A site plan allows you to view in advance the effect a new structure will have when finished. It is important to conceptualize how the new addition blends in with property lines, utilities, other structures, permanent mature plants, land contours and roads. You also need to be certain of the visibility of the new structure from vantage points both outside and within your property lines. In addition, a site plan may be required by local building officials.

Tools Checklist

If you are an experienced do-it-yourselfer, you probably have most of the tools needed for any of the projects in this book. If this is your first project, compare the tools you have on hand to the list below. Most are available at rental shops, so you can have "the right tool for the job" without spending a lot of extra money right at first.

Gather together the tools you will need for your project before you begin construction. This simple rule is as important as having your building materials and lumber on site in the needed sizes and quantity before you start. The frustration and aggravation you eliminate will be well worth the time it takes to get organized before you begin.

Your basic tool list should include:

Brushes & rollers to apply finishes	Power drill & screwdriver
Carpenter's level	Power jigsaw
Carpenter's square	Shovel
Chalk line	Socket set
Chisel	Tape measure
Circular saw	Tool belt
Framing angle	Line level
Hammer	Nail set
Handsaw	Wheelbarrow (to move materials & to mix concrete)
Plumb bob	

Selecting Lumber

Each project in this book has a list of lumber and other building materials required. You will need to determine

and select the type of wood you want to use. Many wood species are used for outdoor structures. For most structures that may be used as living spaces, you'll want to choose a good construction-grade wood. For other structures such as sheds or gazebos you might decide on some of the more common woods, such as redwood, Western Red Cedar, Douglas Fir, Spruce, Southern Yellow Pine, Northern Pine and Ponderosa Pine. Enlist the help of a local lumber supplier when making your final decisions.

> **Lumber that is in contact with, or even in close proximity to, the ground must be decay-resistant.**

One of the primary considerations in selecting the correct lumber for your project is to prevent the base structure from decaying. For this reason, lumber that is in contact with, or even in close proximity to, the ground must be decay-resistant. Select a resistant species or treat your lumber with a preservative before using it in your building or project.

You might want to select pressure-treated wood, which is available from most lumber dealers and home centers. In pressure-treated wood, preservatives or fire-retardant chemicals are forced into the fibers of the lumber to protect and prolong its durability. Although pressure-treated wood seems an obvious choice, some precautions and decisions about its use are warranted. Because of the chemicals used in its treatment, pressure-treated wood should not be used if it will come into direct contact with drinking water or food for humans or animals. Further precautions include: do not use boards with a visible chemical residue; wear a mask and goggles when sawing treated wood; do not burn treated wood; and sweep up and safely dispose of all sawdust and wood scraps. Check with your lumber supplier for additional restrictions and precautions.

Choose a lumber dealer you can rely on to assist you with wood selection—

one who will be familiar with the lumber commonly used in your area for garages and other outdoor buildings. Be sure what you want is available locally. If you desire a wood type that is not normally in stock in your part of the country, you'll pay much more to acquire it.

SITE PREPARATION

At last, it's time to begin! You've selected the site according to your observations and site plan; you've obtained complete project plans; you've secured all permits; and you've gathered together all code-approved materials and required tools. Now, to help assure success, follow these important steps so construction will proceed quickly and without too many hitches.

Drainage: This is an important word to remember when you begin construction. Water must drain away from the foundation or it will pool on structural supports, eventually rotting and weakening them. And, water saturated soil beneath footings may not remain firm enough to support the structure.

The easiest way to supply drainage is to slope the ground away from your structure so water will run off naturally. If the ground does not slope naturally, dig a drainage channel or channels to carry water away. Notice where water runoff flows naturally and install trenches there.

If runoff is light, dig trenches about 1 foot deep and line with 1 to 2 inches of gravel. If possible, direct the runoff downhill into irrigation wells for trees and shrubs. This form of water harvesting has dual benefits: it takes care of excess water and it supplies plants with needed moisture.

If runoff is heavy, further engineering will be required, such as laying perforated pipe, or lining the trenches with concrete. Consult with an architect or engineer to see if these or additional methods are required to handle heavy runoff.

Remove weeds and turf: Getting weeds out of the way before you begin to build makes construction easier. Hoe or pull out weeds in small areas. In larger areas, a small cultivator can be used to turn over the soil. Keep cultivation shallow or weed seeds will be brought up to the soil surface to germinate.

> **Water must drain away from the foundation or it will pool on structural supports, eventually weakening them.**

To prevent future weed growth, lay down heavy black plastic sheeting (at least 6 mils thick). Newly available "fabric mulch" is also good for this purpose. It prevents weed growth, yet allows water to pass through and soak into the soil, which results in less runoff downgrade. Cover the sheeting or mulch with about 2 inches of pea gravel to hold it in place.

PROJECT LAYOUT

A simple surveying procedure allows you to be sure your project will be built square, with true 90-degree angles. Batter boards are used to square the starting corner of your project. This corner could be the outside wall of the foundation or the center point of your first post. The first step is to construct a right triangle using the "3-4-5 Method" described below. (Actually, any multiple of 3-4-5, such as 6-8-10, or 12-16-20 will work—the larger the better.)

The 3-4-5 Method

Using stakes and string, run a line (Line One) parallel to what you have determined will be the front of your project. Install batter boards as shown in Illustration A (see below) and attach string. Be sure the batter boards are far enough apart to build your project between. Install a second set of batter boards perpendicular to Line One and attach Line Two. Using a length of string or a measuring tape, measure 4 feet along Line One from the point where it intersects Line Two. Mark that point with a piece of string that will slide. Measure 3 feet along Line Two from the Line One/Line Two intersec-

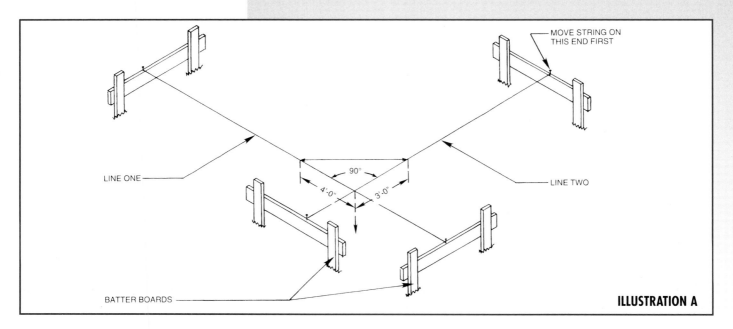

LINE ONE

MOVE STRING ON THIS END FIRST

90°

4'-0" 3'-0"

LINE TWO

BATTER BOARDS

ILLUSTRATION A

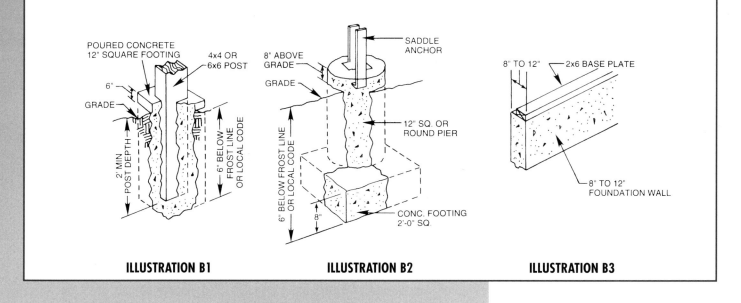

POURED CONCRETE 12" SQUARE FOOTING
4x4 OR 6x6 POST
6"
GRADE
2' MIN POST DEPTH
6" BELOW FROST LINE OR LOCAL CODE

ILLUSTRATION B1

SADDLE ANCHOR
8" ABOVE GRADE
GRADE
12" SQ. OR ROUND PIER
6" BELOW FROST LINE OR LOCAL CODE
8"
CONC. FOOTING 2'-0" SQ.

ILLUSTRATION B2

8" TO 12"
2x6 BASE PLATE
8" TO 12" FOUNDATION WALL

ILLUSTRATION B3

tion point and mark it with a piece of string that will slide. Next, measure 3 feet along Line Two from the Line One/Line Two intersection and mark it in the same manner. Now, measure the distance across from the string you tied to Line One to the string on Line Two. The corner is exactly square when this distance is five feet.

Adjust the string on the far end of Line Two and slide the string on Line One until the measurements equal the correct ratio. Double-check the accuracy by placing a carpenter's square in the corner. This process will establish a point with a perfect 90-degree angle from which to begin building your project. Regardless of where the point is it will become the main reference point for the entire project.

FOUNDATIONS, FOOTINGS AND PIERS

A poor foundation can ruin even the best project. Illustration B presents three options for a foundation, using piers and a poured concrete wall on a footer. Other methods include a concrete block foundation wall, or even placing your structure directly on precast concrete piers.

Local codes vary in requirements for footing sizes and depths. If you are in an area where the ground freezes, footings must be placed at the code-recommended depth below the soil level.

Be sure to check the codes in your area before installing the footings for your project.

Piers, footings and foundations are the base of any project. Piers are formed from concrete, either pre-cast or "pour-your-own." To pour your own, either build your own forms from lumber, or use the ready-made forms of wax-impregnated cardboard, available in cylinder or block shapes, at local home-improvement or lumber supply stores.

To build a foundation wall, you must first pour the footing. A trench is dug below the frost line to the required dimensions of the footing. The footing is usually 8" to 10" deep by 16" to 20" wide. Once the concrete has set, build the foundation wall forms on top of the footing. The concrete is poured between the forms. An optional method is to set a block foundation wall on top of the footing. Pre-cast piers are available in various sizes and with drift-pin connections. These can be set on grade or sunken into the ground, depending on the type you select.

ATTACH PROJECT TO FOUNDATION

Whether your project is sitting on posts or a foundation wall, all wood within 12 inches of the soil should be treated as required by most codes. Illustrations B1 and B2 show the two most common ways to attach a post to a

footing or pier. By setting metal connectors in poured concrete you will create a strong connection less susceptible to wood rot than simply sinking a post in concrete. All connectors should be of the highest quality 16- to 18-gauge hot-dipped galvanized steel. Ensure that all nails, bolts, nuts and other fittings exposed to the elements are also of galvanized steel.

> **All connectors should be of the highest quality 16- to 18-gauge hot-dipped galvanized steel.**

Illustration B3 shows the base plate on the top of the trench footing secured with anchor bolts.

Many additional foundation options are available, such as slab flooring with anchor ties, block walls and others. The one you need will be indicated in the detailed set of plans for each project.

Leveling Post Height

If you are pouring a foundation wall or laying block, the top should be perfectly level for placing the sill plate. Since posts set in or on top of a footing or pier may vary in height, follow these guidelines. Use a post 6 inches longer than needed to allow for variations. After the concrete has set, string a level line to find the top of the post height needed for your project. Level the posts

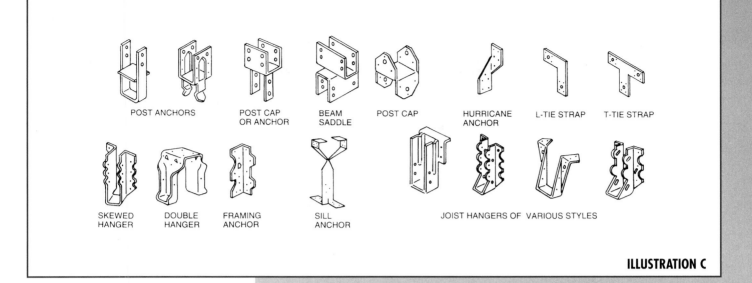

POST ANCHORS   POST CAP OR ANCHOR   BEAM SADDLE   POST CAP   HURRICANE ANCHOR   L-TIE STRAP   T-TIE STRAP

SKEWED HANGER   DOUBLE HANGER   FRAMING ANCHOR   SILL ANCHOR   JOIST HANGERS OF VARIOUS STYLES

ILLUSTRATION C

and cut to the same height prior to attaching floor joists or beams.

Making Framing Connections

Joists, rafters and even sill plate connections can be made stronger by using manufactured metal framing devices. Illustration C shows a variety of connectors and their applications. Other connectors are available which are easy to install and provide a strong connection.

FLOOR CONSTRUCTION

Slab foundations are used for the flooring in most of the structures in this book. If you are building a gazebo or other structure using decking, the joists may attach to the posts or beams with the decking extended to the edge. It may also be modified for railings or columns, as shown in Illustration D.

> **Structures in this book which have an upper level are constructed using conventional western platform techniques.**

Second-Floor Construction

In general, structures in this book which have an upper level are constructed using conventional western platform techniques. Additional bracing can be provided with blocking or cross-bridging. "Blocking" uses boards the same dimension as the joists, placed

between the joists for added support. "Cross-bridging" uses 2x3s or 2x4s placed in an X pattern between joists for added support. If blocking boards are cut precisely to size before joists are installed, they can serve as a measure to ensure correct spacing between joists. Stagger the blocking pattern to make it easier to install.

Be sure all joists are installed at the same level. Because the actual project flooring goes on top of the joists, they must be the same height or the surface of the floor will be uneven. To check, place a line over the joists and pull it tight. It will be easy to tell which joists are too high or too low and need to be adjusted.

Splicing Joists

Joists, like beams, must be spliced when they do not span the entire distance between beams. Splice only above

a beam to ensure needed support. Use a wood or metal cleat, or overlap the joist at the beam. Extend the joint at least 8 or more inches beyond the sides of each beam to increase the strength of the junction and to allow room for the splice.

> **Joists, like beams, must be spliced when they do not span the entire distance between beams.**

If the joist spans over 8 feet, apply a cross-brace or blocking to prevent twisting. The longer the distance, the more likely the joist is to twist. If the floor span of your project is 8 feet or less, the end headers normally provide enough support so that cross-bracing is not required. Use blocking for added support for joists that are 2x4, 2x6, or 2x8, but for joists that are

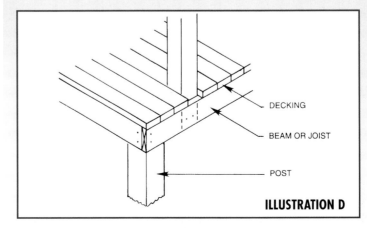

DECKING

BEAM OR JOIST

POST

ILLUSTRATION D

2x10 or larger, install wood or metal cross bracing.

STANDARD WALL CONSTRUCTION

In platform framing, exterior walls and interior partitions have a single 2x4-plate (2x6 when studs are 2x6s) that rests on the subfloor. This is called the bottom or sole plate. The top of the walls have a doubled plate called the top plate, or cap plate, that supports ceiling joists, and, in most cases, roof rafters. The walls of a structure usually are built lying flat on the subfloor, then raised into position in one section. Wall studs are also normally placed 16" on center, but if 2x6 studs are used, then 24" on center may be acceptable.

There are a number of ways to construct the corner post. The method shown in Illustration E is one of the most common. Also shown is a sheet of exterior plywood at the corner. This is used as corner bracing. There are other methods, such as a 2x4 notched at a 45-degree angle, or metal "T" bracing, but using plywood is the easiest and fastest method. For small structures with $\frac{5}{8}$" T-111 siding, or equal, this could also serve as the needed corner bracing and is sufficient for most codes.

Prior to starting the wall construction, be sure to verify all rough opening sizes for doors, windows, etc. All

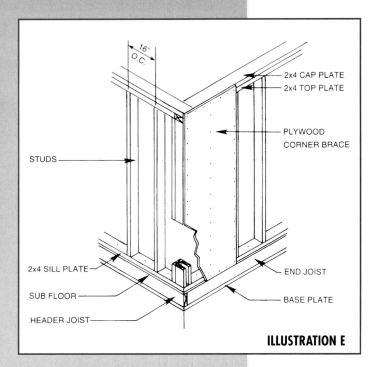

ILLUSTRATION E

headers above the doors and windows are constructed of 2x material, which is really 1½" thick. With two 2x6s or two 2x8s with a ½" plywood spacer, you can build a header to support almost any window or door span for the projects in this book, except garage door headers, in which glue laminated beams are used.

ROOF FRAMING

Up to the cap plate or top plate, the method of construction depends on the type of framing system used. Above

the cap plate, the method of construction depends mainly on the style of the roof indicated for the structure.

> **The two most common roof styles are the gable and the hip.**

Two structures built from identical plans can look considerably different when only the style of the roof is changed. The two most common roof styles are the gable (Illustration F) and

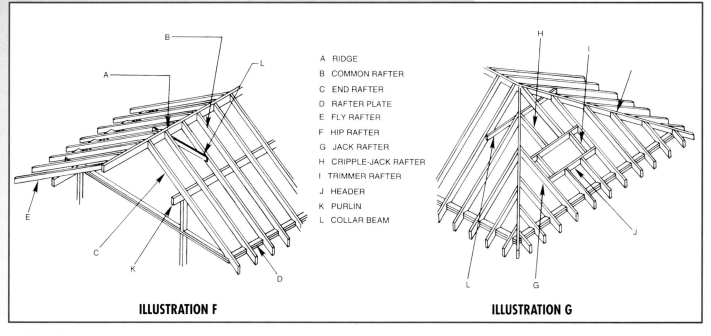

A RIDGE
B COMMON RAFTER
C END RAFTER
D RAFTER PLATE
E FLY RAFTER
F HIP RAFTER
G JACK RAFTER
H CRIPPLE-JACK RAFTER
I TRIMMER RAFTER
J HEADER
K PURLIN
L COLLAR BEAM

ILLUSTRATION F

ILLUSTRATION G

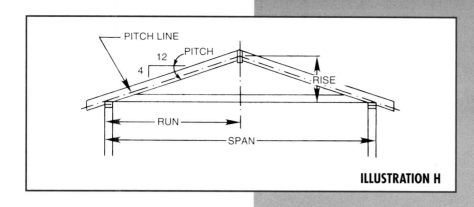

ILLUSTRATION H

the hip (Illustration G), however, other styles are also used, such as a shed roof or gambrel roof, plus variations and combinations of each style.

There are five roof-framing terms you should know, which are used in calculating rafter length: span, rise, run, pitch, and pitch line, as shown in Illustration H. To construct a roof you will need to use a rafter square, available from local suppliers. Get either a metal angle or a triangular square. The least expensive model is a plastic triangular square. It comes with instructions on how to use it to measure rafters, cut angles, and cut "the bird's mouth," which is the part that sits on the wall cap plate. Because cutting the roof rafters is probably the most difficult task involved in building a garden structure, the rafter square is the most useful tool you can have.

STAIRS AND STEPS

Many projects require stairs and steps to provide exits to ground level or to upper-level living quarters. Stairs are composed of the tread, the surface you walk on, and the riser, the vertical distance between steps. Stairs are a minimum of 3 feet wide. It is important that you retain a constant riser-to-tread ratio. This ensures an equal distance

between steps to avoid missteps and stumbles. A common riser-to-tread ratio is 6:12, which can be built by using two 2x6 treads and a 2x6 riser. For example, if the width of the tread is 12 inches, the next step should "rise" 6 inches.

The supports to which the steps are attached are called stair stringers or carriage, usually built from 2x12s. Steps can also be constructed as a single step from floor to ground, or from one floor level to another. Some steps are constructed as a separate level, a kind of continuous step, from one floor level to another. Illustration I shows the options for stringers and treads, plus a chart indicating standard tread-riser ratios.

INSULATION

If you are going to heat or cool your structure, you may want to insulate the walls and ceiling. If so, the normal wall insulation is R-19 in cold climates, with R-38 for the ceiling. R-values vary according to climate, so check with your local supplier for the requirements in your area.

RECOMMENDED READING

Residential Framing, by William P. Spence, Sterling Publishing Co.

Graphic Guide to Frame Construction, by Rob Thallon, The Taunton Press. ◀

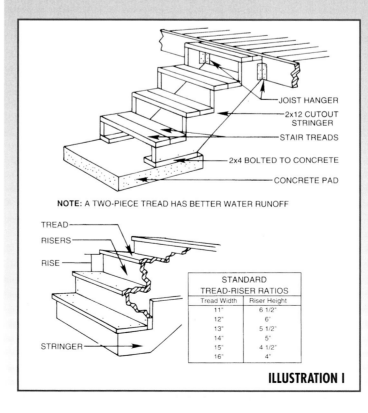

STANDARD TREAD-RISER RATIOS	
Tread Width	Riser Height
11"	6 1/2"
12"	6"
13"	5 1/2"
14"	5"
15"	4 1/2"
16"	4"

ILLUSTRATION I

GLOSSARY

Anchor bolt: A device for connecting wood members to concrete or masonry.

Blocking: Used for added support for floor joists and to prevent twisting.

Balustrade: A complete handrail assembly. Includes rails, balusters, subrails and fillets.

Batter board: Simple wooden forms used early in construction to mark the corners of the structure and the height of foundation walls.

Beam: A horizontal framing member of wood or steel, no less than 5 inches thick and at least 2 inches wider than it is thick.

Board: Any piece of lumber more than 1 inch wide, but less than 2 inches wider in thickness.

Common rafter: Any of several identical structural members of a roof that run at right angles to walls and end at right angles to main roof framing members.

Concrete: A mixture of cement, sand, gravel and water.

Cross-bridging: Diagonal wood braces that form an "X" between floor joists.

Drip edge: A strip of metal used to protect the edges of a roof structure from water damage.

Drywall: A method of covering wall and ceiling surfaces with dry materials, rather than wet materials such as plaster. Refers primarily to the application of gypsum wallboard, also called drywall.

Edge joist: The outer joist of a floor or ceiling system that runs parallel to other joists. See *header joist*.

Foundation: The part of a building that rests on a footing and supports all of the structure above it.

Frame: The wood skeleton of a building. Also called framing.

Header: Any structural wood member used across the ends of an opening to support the cut ends of shortened framing members in a floor, wall or roof.

Header joist: The outer joist of a floor or ceiling system that runs across other joists. See *edge joist*.

Joist: A horizontal structural member that, together with other similar members, supports a floor or ceiling system.

O.C.: Abbreviation for On Centers, a measurement from one center line to the next, usually of structural members.

Ridgeboard: The horizontal board at the ridge to which the top ends of rafters are attached. Also called a ridge beam or ridge pole.

GARAGES

The Suburban

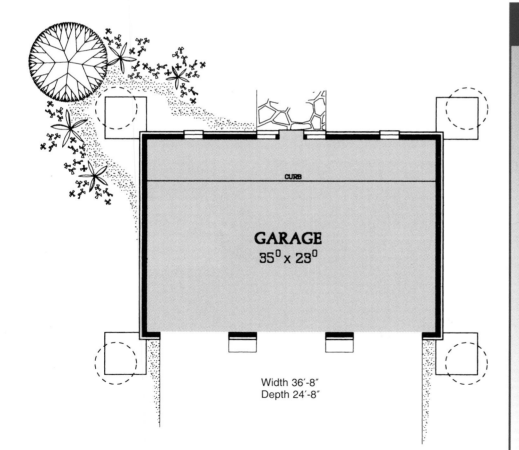

CURB

GARAGE
35⁰ x 23⁰

Width 36′-8″
Depth 24′-8″

PLAN G201

▶ Nestled at the back of your property or located adjacent to the main house, this spacious, 294-square-foot, hip-roof garage provides shelter and security for one, two, or three vehicles. A raised curb, stretching the entire 36'-8" width, can be used to accommodate a workbench for small projects. Or, because of proximity and access to the back yard through an exterior door, the curb area is a natural for a potting bench. The addition of brick and masonry planters at each outside corner of the garage adds architectural interest and softens the lines of this straightforward design. Design by Home Planners

The Versatile

PLAN G255

▶ Is it a garage? Is it a workshop? The answer is both. You can put this 900-square-foot area to work however it suits you best—and modify the exterior to match your house. Providing space enough for three cars is only the first benefit. Convert the third parking bay to an optional work pit—perfect for the devoted mechanic's do-it-yourself car maintenance. A generous work area adjacent to the parking bay allows space for a counter, air compressor, welders, and other tool-time essentials. The back wall storage area includes optional cabinets and a wash sink, with handy side-door access for bringing the mower and other yard equipment in out of the weather.

To vary the exterior appearance of this multi-use garage, select Plan G254, The Shadows, with angled masonry trim for a tailored look. Add stone or brick quoins to the exterior corners and choose a wider block pattern for the doors for the solid look of The Stonecutter, Plan G256. Or, choose the lighter, airy look of Plan G257, The Breezeway, using horizontal wood siding and decorative, diamond-shape panels in the doors. Design by Home Planners

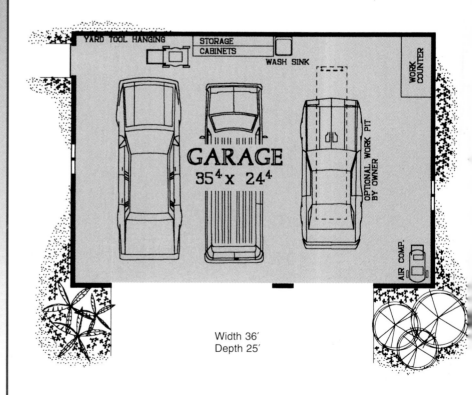

Width 36'
Depth 25'

Plan G254

Plan G256

Plan G257

The Practical

PLAN G104

▶ Large, attractive panels march across the front of this 816-square-foot, three-car garage, with shingled hip-roof. Definition and color are added with gently curved masonry walls and bracketed sconces. Windows in each side wall provide natural light and cross-ventilation when the garage doors are closed. A workbench and storage area line the back wall along with easy access through a single exterior door. Design by Home Planners

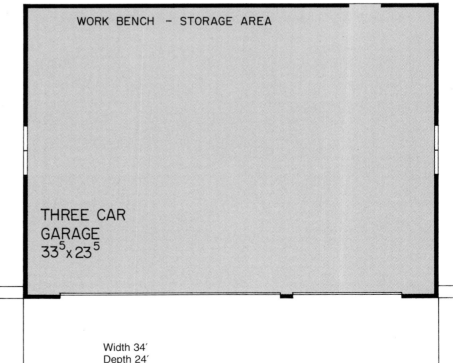

WORK BENCH – STORAGE AREA

THREE CAR
GARAGE
$33^5 \times 23^5$

Width 34'
Depth 24'

The Convertible

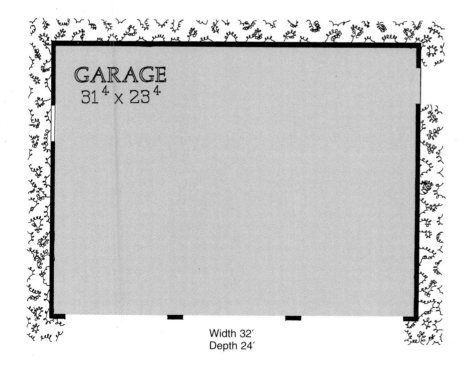

GARAGE
31⁴ x 23⁴

Width 32'
Depth 24'

PLAN G123

▶ Three 9' x 7' garage doors convert this 768-square-foot area equally well to private or commercial use. Vary the selection of siding and doorjambs on this wide-gable-roof structure to blend with the style of your home. For use on a commercial site, choose the options for electric outlets in each bay area. Plenty of room is provided along the 32' back wall for a workbench and a storage area. A pre-hung steel door at the back side wall allows convenient entry and exit. Design by Home Planners

The Square Cut

PLAN 8974

▶ A neat 23'-4" x 23'-4", this compact two-car garage will make the most of the space available, plus add a decorative accent to your main house. The gabled roof can support a mixed design of shingles to complement your choice of siding and garage doors. An easy-access exterior door in the sidewall and a curb along the back for storage or work area add to this structure's usefulness. Design by Larry W. Garnett and Associates, Inc.

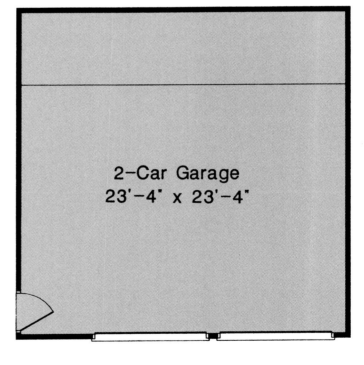

2-Car Garage
23'-4" x 23'-4"

Width 24'
Depth 24'

The Fanciful

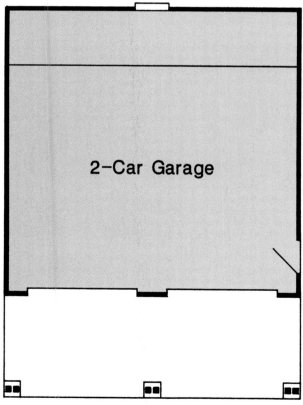

2-Car Garage

Width 24'
Depth 31'

PLAN 8972

▶ Go creative! Much more than protection for two cars, this nifty little number is full of surprises. The gable roof sports an intersecting overhang to form an 8'-foot shaded area supported by three brick-and-pillar columns with decorative arched trim. A double-hung sash window front and center, complete with shutters, adds natural light and lots of appeal. A one-more-for-good-measure triangle of trim above the window, and a side door for easy access make this plan all but irresistible. Additional light is provided through clear panels on the garage doors and a window in the back wall. Design by Larry W. Garnett and Associates, Inc.

Sunrise, Sunset

PLAN G297

▶ Taking its name from the sunburst pattern in the wide door panels, this two-car garage also accommodates adequate storage areas for tools, yard and gardening equipment, and recycling and trash bins. A 16' x 7' garage door provides safe passage for your vehicles and an exterior door at the back of the side wall offers easy access to the storage areas.

If a clean line is the look you're after, select The Greystone (G294), for its off-set masonry trim. Paint a sophisticated gray and white, or go modern with a wild array of color. For country charm, The Sunnyside (G295), will go a long way toward enhancing a rural setting with its shingled roof (red, maybe?) and a weathervane perched atop a louvered cupola. The Cornerstone (G296), offers an accent on detail by combining stone quoins with vertical and horizontal brick trim. Choose a bold, rectangular block pattern for the 16' x 7" garage door to complete the solid look. Design by Home Planners

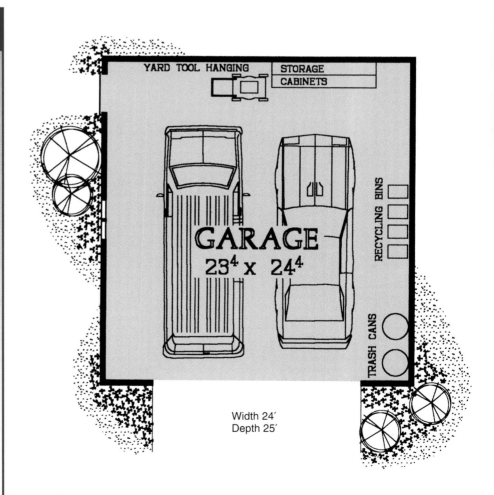

Width 24'
Depth 25'

Plan G294

Plan G295

Plan G296

Simplicity

PLAN G102

▶ The high-pitched roof of this free-standing, 528-square-foot garage shelters two cars, plus room enough for a work-bench and welcome extra storage. Slotted shutters on the opposing double-hung windows are repeated in miniature to flank the louvered vent at the peak of the roofline. Wide wood trim around the recessed-pattern garage door creates a clean, un-cluttered line. Design by Home Planners

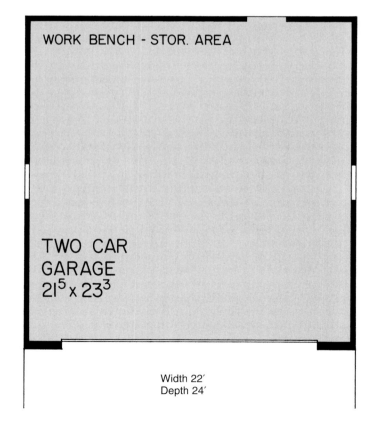

WORK BENCH - STOR. AREA

TWO CAR
GARAGE
$21^5 \times 23^3$

Width 22′
Depth 24′

The Monroe

GARAGE
27⁵ x 27⁵

Width 28′
Depth 28′

PLAN G125

▶ Deep eaves and vertical, wide-panel siding offer a no-nonsense approach to this 784-square-foot, two-car garage with generous work area. Enter by either of the 9' x 7' garage doors, or by the pre-hung steel door in the back side wall. Natural light is provided through translucent panels in the garage doors. Conveniently placed electric outlets in each parking bay and two in the back wall increase the versatility of this multi-use structure. This plan is the same as G119 on page 23, but has slightly larger dimensions. Design by Home Planners

The Compact

PLAN G105

▶ A wide-gable roofline provides a generous overhang on all sides of this compact garage with a single 16' x 7' garage door flanked by exterior lights. The 484-square-foot floor plan allows space for a workbench and storage area along the back wall. A double-hung window along the side wall provides natural light, while an exterior door in the back wall provides easy access to the work and storage area. Design by Home Planners

WORK BENCH – STOR. AREA

TWO CAR
GARAGE
$21^5 \times 21^5$

Width 22'
Depth 22'

The Madison

GARAGE
23⁵ x 23⁵

Width 24′
Depth 24′

PLAN G119

▶ With the same basic specs as Plan G125 on page 21, Plan G119 provides a garage with slightly smaller overall dimensions. Deep eaves and wide panel siding offer a no-nonsense approach to this 784-square-foot, two-car garage with generous work area. Enter by either of the 9′ x 7′ garage doors, or by the pre-hung steel door in the back side wall. Natural light is provided through translucent panels in the garage doors. Conveniently placed electric outlets in each parking bay and two in the back wall increase the versatility of this multi-use structure. Design by Home Planners

Coach House

PLAN G101

▶ Notched corners on the steeply pitched roof of this wood-shingled garage enhance the wrought-iron exterior lights on each side of the 17' x 7' door. The 528-square-foot area provides plenty of room for two cars, plus a workbench and storage area. Opposing double-hung windows in the side walls are neatly framed with shutters and louvered vents in the gable peak allow for controlled air flow. Design by Home Planners

WORK BENCH - STOR. AREA

TWO CAR
GARAGE
$21^5 \times 23^3$

Width 22'
Depth 24'

The Transition

GARAGE
23⁵ x 23⁵

Width 24'
Depth 24'

▶ Intended to be versatile, this 784-square-foot, two-car garage with deep eaves and wide-panel siding offers a generous work area. Enter by either of the 9' x 7' garage doors, or by the pre-hung steel door in the back side wall. Natural light is provided through translucent panels in the garage doors. Conveniently placed electric outlets in each parking bay and two in the back wall increase the versatility of this multi-use structure. Design by Home Planners

GARAGES

The Brickster

PLAN 8977

▶ A good choice for cold climates, the steep pitch of this hip-roof design will stop snow build-up cold. The solid brick construction topped with decorative shingles offers enough space to get two cars in out of the weather. Natural light enters through a double-hung window in the side wall, and side entry is provided by a pre-hung door near the front…just a short dash to the house. Design by Larry W. Garnett and Associates, Inc.

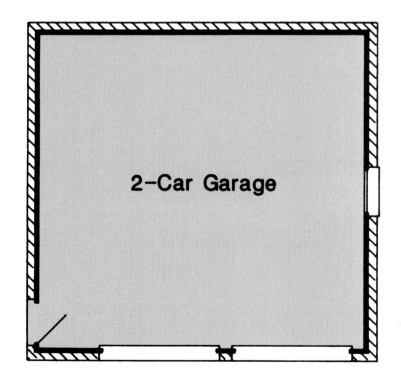

2-Car Garage

Width 24'
Depth 23'

Showtime

PLAN G122

▶ Ready to suit your needs, this garage has 768 square feet of usable space. Intended to provide shelter and security for two cars, this garage also offers four conveniently placed electric outlets to expand your options. A large work area at the rear of this 24' x 32' structure is accessed through a pre-hung steel door at the rear of the side wall. This plan has the same basic configuration as G119 (page 23) and G125 (page 21), but is much deeper than either. Design by Home Planners

GARAGE
23⁵ x 31⁵

Width 24'
Depth 32'

One Car, Plus

PLAN G103

▶ Store your car and your bike, or your car and your motorcycle, plus have room left over for a workbench and generous storage areas. The 385-square-foot floor plan has a curbed work area at the back with 14 feet of garage storage. Additional storage is provided in a second area—4' x 11'-5"—adjacent to the garage door. Both storage areas are easy to reach through an exterior side door. Natural light enters through a double-hung window in the 24' side wall. Design by Home Planners

WORK BENCH - STOR. AREA

CURB

1½ CAR GARAGE 13⁵x23⁵

STOR. AREA 4⁰x11⁵

CURB

Width 18'
Depth 24'

The Adjustable

GARAGE
15^5 x 19^5

(G116)
Width 16'
Depth 20'

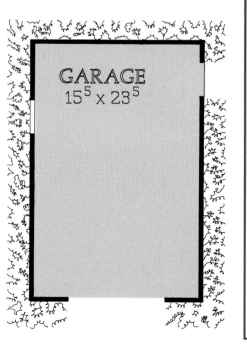

GARAGE
15^5 x 23^5

(G117)
Width 16'
Depth 24'

PLANS G116 & G117

▶ Let the size of your lot dictate how large you decide to make this functional single-car garage. Plan G116 is 16' x 20' with 320 square feet of usable area, and Plan G117 adds an additional 4' to the depth for 384 square feet of area. Choose a garage door style with clear panels to provide natural light. Optional electric service in the center of the parking bay adds versatility to the many uses of this sturdy structure. A wide, gable roofline and vertical siding allow this design to blend easily with many traditional and contemporary house styles. Access to the storage in the back is through a pre-hung exterior door in the side wall. Design by Home Planners

Victoria

PLAN G289

▶ An amazing array of shingles, millwork and decorative touches is incorporated in the exterior design of this Victorian garage and guest cottage. The first-floor garage space is identical to the mechanic's garage shown on page 12, but in this version we've added a second-floor guest apartment. A fully equipped kitchen is on the right, and ahead is a generous living room with built-in bookshelves and a tempting window seat in the dormer window. A full bath, with a shower, linen closet and laundry facilities, adds to the functional floor plan. A large bedroom features sloping ceilings and a welcome walk-in closet. Choose one of the facades on the opposite page for a different look. Design by Home Planners

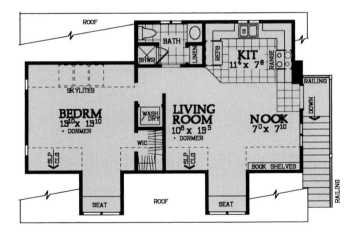

ROOF

BATH

SHWR LINEN REFG KIT 11⁴ x 7⁸ RANGE

RAILING

SKYLITES

BEDRM 13¹⁰ x 13¹⁰ + DORMER

WASH DRY

LIVING ROOM 10⁶ x 19⁵ + DORMER

NOOK 7⁰ x 7¹⁰

DOWN

WIC

SLP CLG

SLP CLG

BOOK SHELVES

RAILING

SEAT

ROOF

SEAT

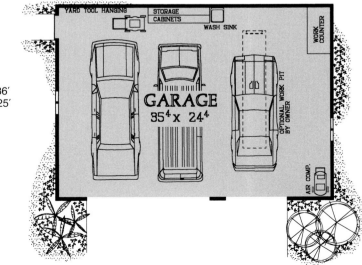

Width 36'
Depth 25'

YARD TOOL HANGING   STORAGE CABINETS   WASH SINK   WORK COUNTER

GARAGE 35⁴ x 24⁴

OPTIONAL WORK PIT BY OWNER

AIR COMP.

Plan 288

Plan 287

Plan 286

Hidden Loft

PLAN G206

▶ Attractive and functional, this impressive structure has room for three cars in the garage section and 670 square feet of living area—complete with kitchen, bathroom, bookshelves and closet —to use as a studio or a hideaway loft for guests. The treatment of the steeply pitched gable roof is repeated in three gabled dormers, each with tall narrow windows framed with shutters. Access to the second-floor loft area is by a railed exterior stairway which leads to a small landing with its own covered roof supported by wooden columns. The clipped corners of the trim around each of the three car bays lends country charm. Four wrought-iron coach lights complete the effect. Design by Home Planners

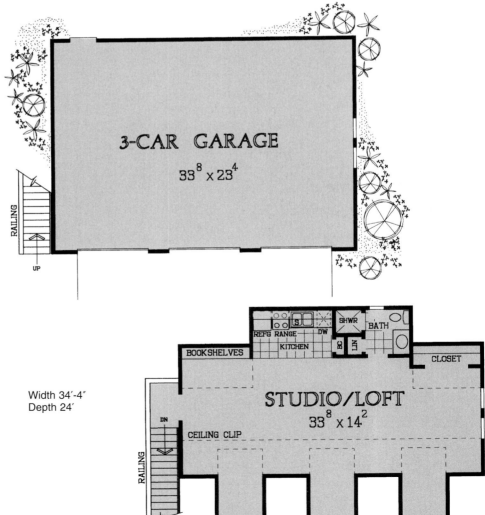

Width 34'-4"
Depth 24'

Grand View

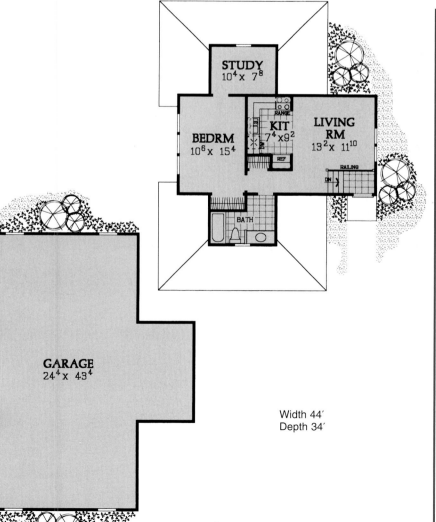

STUDY
10⁴ x 7⁸

BEDRM
10⁶ x 15⁴

KIT
7⁴ x 9²

RANGE

DW

REF

LIVING
RM
13² x 11¹⁰

RAILING

DN

BATH

GARAGE
24⁴ x 43⁴

Width 44′
Depth 34′

PLAN G302

▶ Almost too grand to be a mere garage, this design provides enough space for three vehicles, plus a handy work area at the garage level. The second-floor apartment weighs in at a sizable 688 square feet and allows for a large living room, a serviceable kitchen, a bedroom with a full bath and even a study. Use it for frequent guests, a mother-in-law suite or even as a home office. The exterior of this garage fits nicely with almost any style of home, but will work especially well with European, Southwestern, or Mediterranean designs. Design by Home Planners.

Twin Peaks

PLAN 8988

▶ Looking like anything but a three-car garage, this plan features a standard entry set back and is accented with a porch with a covered roof all its own supported by turned wooden posts. Interior stairs are placed between a generous utility room and separate workshop area, with an interior door leading from the stairwell into the garage and an exterior door leading outdoors from the backwall of the garage. Upstairs is a 12'-4" x 13'-4" living room and a 11'-4" x 11'-4" bedroom plus full bath, kitchen, storage and bookshelves. Lighting the living area is a long row of clerestory windows! And downstairs, of course, is a three-car garage. Design by Larry W. Garnett and Associates, Inc.

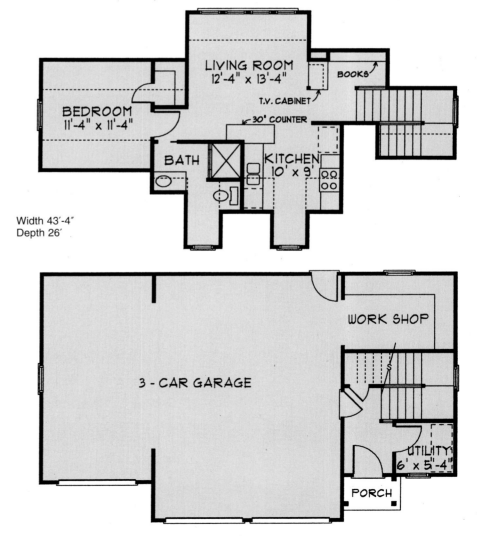

Width 43'-4"
Depth 26'

The Turnabout

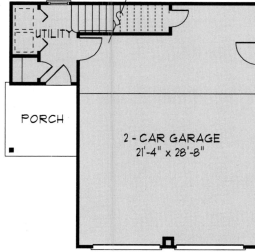

UTILITY

PORCH

2 - CAR GARAGE
21'-4" x 28'-8"

Width 30'-6"
Depth 29'-4'

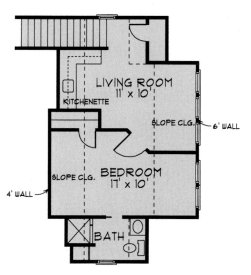

LIVING ROOM
11' x 10'

KITCHENETTE

SLOPE CLG.   6' WALL

SLOPE CLG.   BEDROOM
17' x 10'

4' WALL

BATH

PLAN 9193

▶ Approach from either of the sides and this deceptive design looks like a guest cottage. Approach from the driveway and it is a two-car garage. The attractive modified gable roof covers 553 square feet of living area on the second floor. Interior stairs lead from the laundry area off the two-car garage to the 11' x 10' living room and the 17' x 10' bedroom, both with sloped ceilings. A kitchenette and full bath make this an attractive option for guests or a teenager ready to leave home…but not too far. A row of five second-story windows and a sheltered porch area complete this unique design. Design by Larry W. Garnett and Associates, Inc.

The Studio

PLAN G106

▶ Winner of the Best Use of Space Award! This design provides protection for two cars, plus a 23'-4" x 13'-2" second-floor studio with three-quarter bath and storage in just 428 square feet. Entry to the second floor is via an exterior railed stairway with roofed landing. Two gable-roofed dormers and two windows in the side wall provide plenty of light for arts and crafts and plenty of space for the college set to toss sleeping bags for a weekend visit. Access the garage through two wide doors, or through a standard entry door with a porch at the back wall. Design by Home Planners

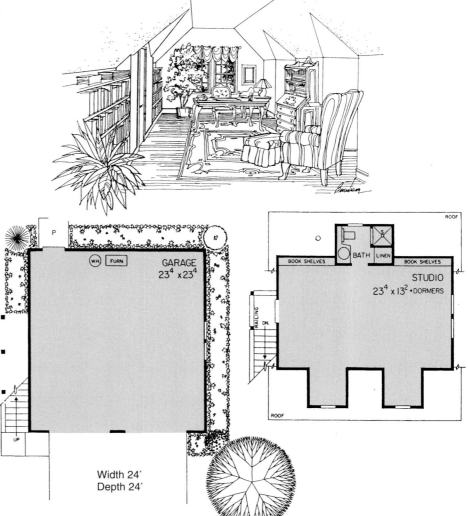

Width 24'
Depth 24'

Great Guest Cottage

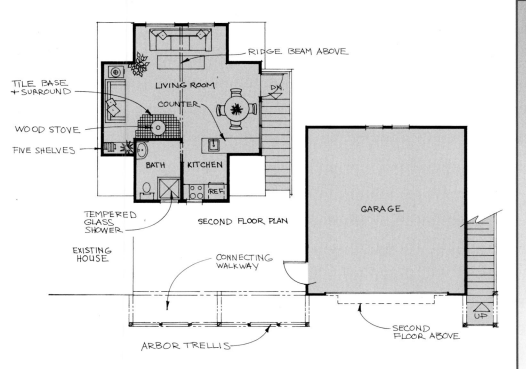

RIDGE BEAM ABOVE

TILE BASE + SURROUND

WOOD STOVE

FIVE SHELVES

LIVING ROOM

COUNTER

DN.

BATH

KITCHEN

REF.

TEMPERED GLASS SHOWER

SECOND FLOOR PLAN

EXISTING HOUSE

CONNECTING WALKWAY

GARAGE

ARBOR TRELLIS

SECOND FLOOR ABOVE

UP

Width 25'
Depth 22'

PLAN R128

▶ At the end of a trellised arbor is this stunning studio/garage. Like the carriage houses of old, there is storage for vehicles on the ground level and snug living quarters on the second level. A box bay projecting over the garage door adds interest to the front elevation. An arbor leads past the garage and up a stairway to a studio apartment hideaway. The high, open living space features a romantic wood stove. Bracketing the living space is a cozy sitting area on one side and a small kitchen and a bath on the other. Design by Home Planners

GARAGES WITH GUEST QUARTERS AND OTHER AMENITIES

The Efficiency

PLAN 8920

▶ This sturdy brick structure provides space in the garage for two cars and a snug little 364-square-foot apartment on the second floor. The second floor is accessed by an interior stairwell and features living accommodations for a guest or college-age child. Two gable-roofed dormers and two side windows provide natural light and fresh air throughout the 21' x 13'-8" living area, full bath, and kitchenette. Design by Larry W. Garnett and Associates, Inc.

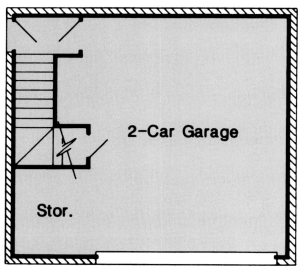

Width 26'
Depth 23'

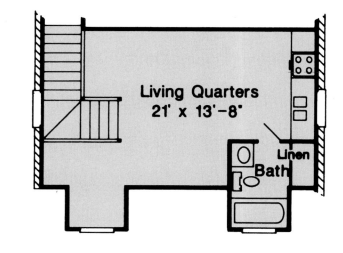

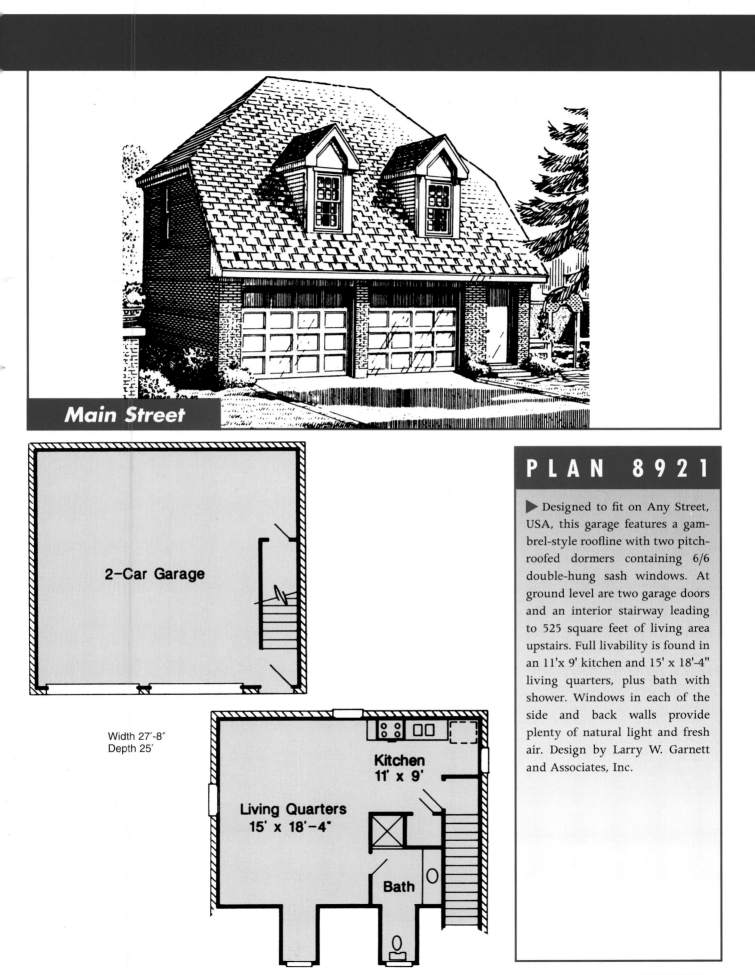

Main Street

2-Car Garage

Width 27'-8"
Depth 25'

Living Quarters
15' x 18'-4"

Kitchen
11' x 9'

Bath

▶ Designed to fit on Any Street, USA, this garage features a gambrel-style roofline with two pitch-roofed dormers containing 6/6 double-hung sash windows. At ground level are two garage doors and an interior stairway leading to 525 square feet of living area upstairs. Full livability is found in an 11'x 9' kitchen and 15' x 18'-4" living quarters, plus bath with shower. Windows in each of the side and back walls provide plenty of natural light and fresh air. Design by Larry W. Garnett and Associates, Inc.

The Cottage

PLAN 7000

▶ The steeply pitched roof and perky single dormer make this floor plan look as though it is just waiting for Hansel and Gretel. Follow the breadcrumbs to the generous 9'-4" x 17' guest quarters on the second floor, where you'll find a bath with a shower and a linen closet. Downstairs there is space for two cars, plus a 6'-8" x 10' workshop and a 6' x 9'-8" utility room and more—a half-bath tucked under the stairs. Double-hung, recessed, 6/6 sash windows add to the charming effect. Design by Larry W. Garnett and Associates, Inc.

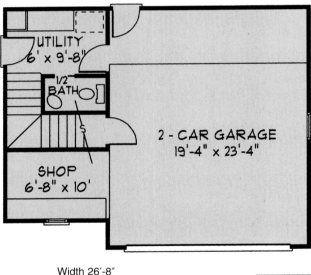

UTILITY
6' x 9'-8"

1/2 BATH

SHOP
6'-8" x 10'

2 - CAR GARAGE
19'-4" x 23'-4"

Width 26'-8"
Depth 24'

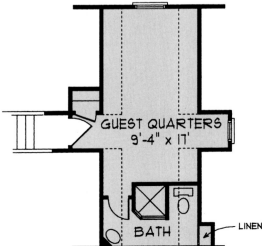

GUEST QUARTERS
9'-4" x 17'

BATH

LINEN

The Plantsman

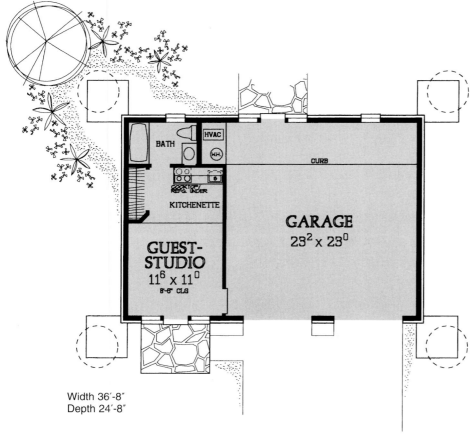

BATH

HVAC

W.H.

COOKTOP/
REFG UNDER

KITCHENETTE

CURB

GARAGE
23^2 x 23^0

GUEST-
STUDIO
11^6 x 11^0
8'-6" CLG

Width 36'-8"
Depth 24'-8"

PLAN G201A

▶ Planters at each corner of the hipped-roof overhang get both sun and shade and soften the lines of this Prairie-style double garage plus guest apartment. Tall, narrow fixed glass windows flank the glass door to the apartment area. Inside is room enough for an 11'-6" x 11' living area or studio, with kitchenette and full bath. The 23'-2" x 23' garage has twin doors, plus an exterior door in the back wall. There is also space for a large storage area along the back wall. This plan is a variation of Plan G201 on page 11. Design by Home Planners

The Ramada

PLAN 8978

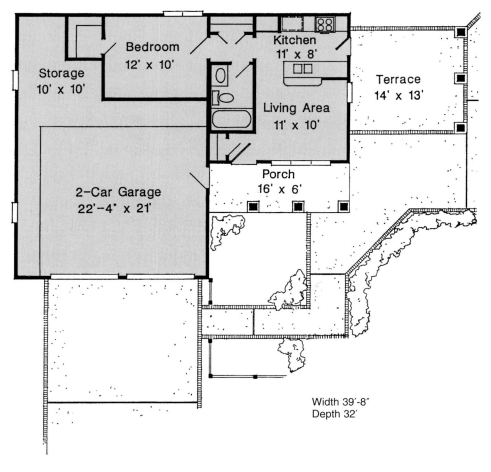

▶ This outstanding structure maximizes living space by providing a shaded 16' x 6' porch in front and, extending from the side wall, a 14' x 13' brick-lined terrace with ramada-style roof overhead. Six wood columns provide the roof support for these lovely outdoor-living areas. Decorative arched vents at the roof peaks of the main structure—plus eight sidewall windows in all—allow for plenty of natural ventilation. Inside, the garage area has space for two cars plus a 10' x 10' storage area. Behind and adjacent to the garage walls is a 468-square-foot living area containing a 12' x 10' bedroom, an 11' x 10' living area, an 11' x 8' kitchen and a full bath, plus lots of closets. The addition of decorative brick trim to walkways and borders adds a polished accent overall. Design by Larry W. Garnett and Associates, Inc.

Width 39'-8"
Depth 32'

Second Home

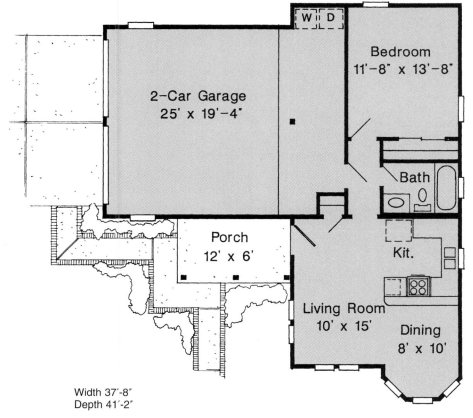

W | D

Bedroom
11'-8" x 13'-8"

2-Car Garage
25' x 19'-4"

Bath

Porch
12' x 6'

Kit.

Living Room
10' x 15'

Dining
8' x 10'

Width 37'-8"
Depth 41'-2"

PLAN 8901

▶ The 25' x 19'-4", two-car garage at the end of the driveway—with generous storage and laundry area—is just for- openers. Wrapped around the back and side of the garage is a 12' x 6' covered porch with a separate entrance which leads to a five-room guest cottage. The 10' x 15' living room opens onto a 8' x 10' dining area with a light and airy bay window. A full-size kitchen, a bath and an 11'-8" x 13'-8" bedroom complete the floor plan. Roomy enough for permanent residence, this functional second home could be connected to the main house with a covered walkway. This could be the ideal solution for having elderly parents near you. Design by Larry W. Garnett and Associates, Inc.

The Consultant

PLAN G285

▶ Need a convenient home office? This well-thought-out floor plan may be the answer. A single 16' x 7' garage door provides shelter for two cars, plus out-of-sight storage areas for yard and garden equipment, garbage cans, and recycling bins. A four-column porch provides entry to the compact apartment or office area. A mini-kitchen (or make this extra work area) and a half-bath with a shower provide added convenience. The bedroom at the back could also be used for additional storage.

Choose The Geometric (Plan G282), The Glitter (Plan G283), or The General (Plan G284) for a different look. Design by Home Planners

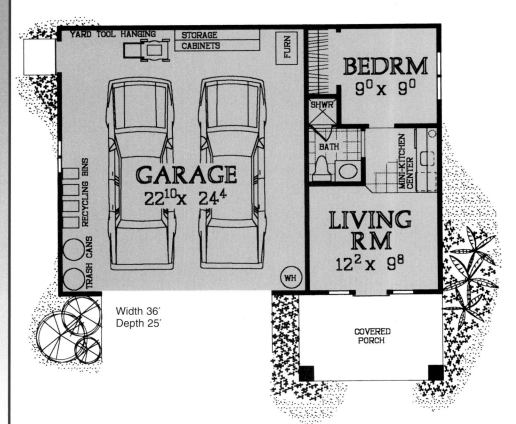

YARD TOOL HANGING

STORAGE CABINETS

FURN

BEDRM
9⁰ x 9⁰

SHWR

BATH

MINI-KITCHEN CENTER

RECYCLING BINS

TRASH CANS

GARAGE
22¹⁰ x 24⁴

LIVING RM
12² x 9⁸

WH

Width 36'
Depth 25'

COVERED PORCH

Plan G282

Plan G283

Plan G284

Double Duty

PLAN G100

▶ The engaging country charm of this two-car garage, plus the functionality of the 431-square-foot, room-to-grow second floor, provide the added space you need. The horizontal clapboard siding of the structure is accented by the vertical panels of the twin garage doors. The modified gambrel-style roof shelters a 16' x 16'-6" living area to use as a future apartment, study, or playroom. It is accessed by interior stairs in the back of the garage. Design by Home Planners

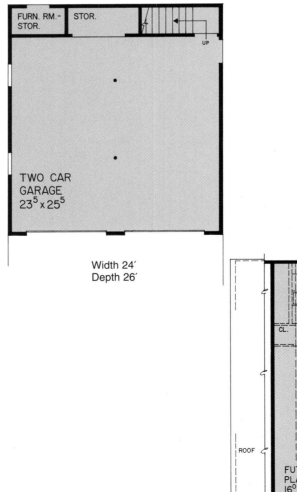

FURN. RM.-STOR.

STOR.

UP

TWO CAR GARAGE 23⁵ x 25⁵

Width 24'
Depth 26'

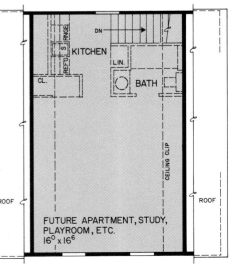

KITCHEN

REF'G. RANGE

LIN.

DN

CL.

BATH

CEILING CLIP

ROOF

ROOF

FUTURE APARTMENT, STUDY, PLAYROOM, ETC. 16⁰ x 16⁶

Second Glance

PLAN G111

▶ The distinctive style of this garage/workshop combination makes you think you are seeing double. The bi-level roofline and wood-and-stone exterior are repeated in exact duplicate, down to the garage door leading into the workshop. With room enough for two cars, the 23' x 23'-4" garage area is flanked by a setback 11'-8" x 19'-4" workshop with a generous storage loft accessed by a ladder. Plenty of natural light is provided through an overhead skylight in the workshop area and additional windows in the back and side walls. Design by Home Planners

DISAPPEARING
STAIRS

LOFT ABOVE

SKYLIGHT

LADDER
LOFT OPENING

WORKSHOP
11⁸ x 19⁴

GARAGE
23⁰ x 23⁴

Width 36′
Depth 24′

Mostly Business

PLAN G265

▶ Greet your clients in the business side of this multi-use structure. There's room enough for a reception/waiting room area in front with an impressive entryway through a four-column porch. Decorative recessed windows flanking the door and two more in the side wall allow for plenty of natural light. In the back is ample space for an office with a storage closet and a bi-fold door. Add a half-bath for maximum convenience.

Choose The Chevron (Plan G262), The Retreat (Plan G264), or The Caprice (Plan G263) for a different look. Design by Home Planners

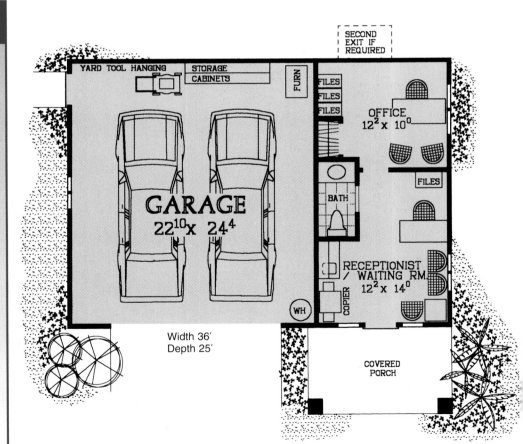

SECOND EXIT IF REQUIRED

YARD TOOL HANGING

STORAGE CABINETS

FURN

FILES
FILES
FILES

OFFICE
12² x 10⁰

FILES

BATH

GARAGE
22¹⁰ x 24⁴

RECEPTIONIST / WAITING RM.
12² x 14⁰

COPIER

WH

Width 36′
Depth 25′

COVERED PORCH

Plan G262

Plan G264

Plan G263

My Workshop

PLAN G279

▶ Behind what looks like another garage door is just what you've always wanted—a fully equipped workshop. Accessed through an 8' x 7' garage door, or from an interior door within the garage itself, is 300 square feet of workshop area. It contains plenty of room for your favorite power tools, work table, storage cabinets, counter space and overhead racks for lumber. On the garage side of this multiuse structure is a two-car garage with a 16' x 7' door. It allows space for yard and garden equipment, plus a convenient area for recycling bins and garbage cans.

Choose The Longview (Plan G280), The Traditional (Plan G278), or The Elite (Plan G281) for a different look. Design by Home Planners

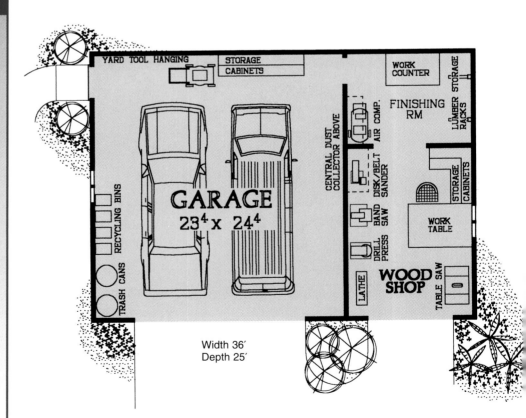

YARD TOOL HANGING | STORAGE CABINETS | WORK COUNTER | STORAGE

RECYCLING BINS

TRASH CANS

GARAGE
23⁴ x 24⁴

CENTRAL DUST COLLECTOR ABOVE

DISK/BELT SANDER | AIR COMP.

FINISHING RM

LUMBER RACKS

BAND SAW

STORAGE CABINETS

DRILL PRESS

WORK TABLE

LATHE

WOOD SHOP

TABLE SAW

Width 36'
Depth 25'

Plan G280

Plan G278

Plan G281

Poolside

PLAN G277

▶ Locate this roomy structure near the pool and provide security for two cars, plus a spacious bathhouse with a changing room and an outdoor patio/lounge area shaded by a generous roof extension. The garage area provides plenty of space to store yard and garden equipment and other necessities like garbage cans and recycling bins. Natural light enters the interior of the changing area through two skylights over the bath and shower area. Built-in benches and counter tops, plus storage and linen closets, offer lots of convenience. The kitchenette is cooled by a ceiling fan and French doors leading to the patio.

Choose The Echo (Plan G276), The Classic (Plan G274), or The Emblem (Plan G275) for a different look. Design by Home Planners

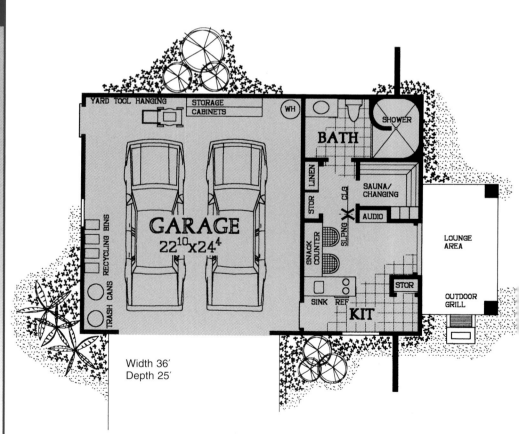

YARD TOOL HANGING
STORAGE CABINETS
WH
SHOWER
BATH
STOR LINEN
SAUNA/ CHANGING
AUDIO
SLPNG CLG
TRASH CANS   RECYCLING BINS
GARAGE
22¹⁰x24⁴
SNACK COUNTER
LOUNGE AREA
STOR
SINK   REF
KIT
OUTDOOR GRILL

Width 36'
Depth 25'

Plan G276

Plan G274

Plan G275

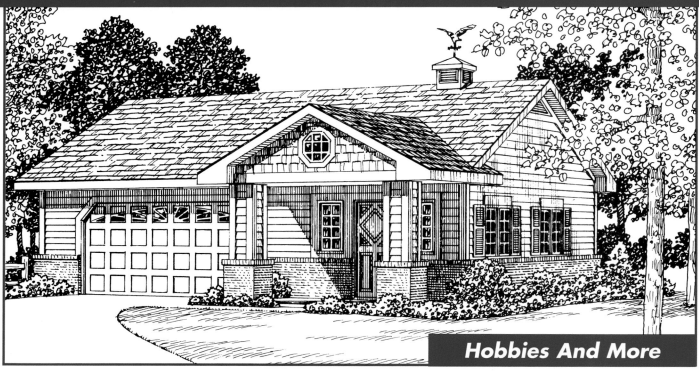

Hobbies And More

PLAN G259

▶ The two-car garage area of this plan provides the basics, but the more than 300 square feet of optional-use area can be transformed into a game room, an exercise room, or a separate space for sewing or other hobbies. Extra convenience is provided by a full bath with a shower and both linen and storage closets. Let your imagination take over when deciding which amenities you need to create a special workspace for your projects. In the garage, you'll find more than enough room for two cars, plus plenty of storage for yard and garden equipment, garbage cans, and recycling bins.

Choose The Club (Plan G258), The Bonus (Plan G260), or The Tiffany (G261) for a different look. Design by Home Planners

STORAGE CABINETS

FURN

SHWR

LINEN

BATH

STORAGE

YARD TOOL HANGING

GARAGE
22¹⁰ x 24⁴

EXERCISE/ SEWING/ HOBBY/ GAME RM
12² x 18²

WH

Width 36'
Depth 25'

COVERED PORCH

Plan G258

Plan G260

Plan G261

Pool Inside

PLAN G272

▶ Two cars and a lap pool all fit inside this 900-square-foot floor plan. If you don't happen to live where it's balmy year 'round, tuck this figure eight-style pool in the 321 square feet to the right of the garage—all under one roof. Access to the pool is through an interior door in the garage, or from outside through its own separate door. Natural light pours into the pool area through four skylights—two on each slope of the roof. The garage has space for two cars with plenty of room left over for storing yard tools, garden equipment, and trash and recycling bins.

Choose Northern Lights (Plan G270), The Fanfare (Plan G271), or The Ivy (Plan G273) for a different look. Design by Home Planners.

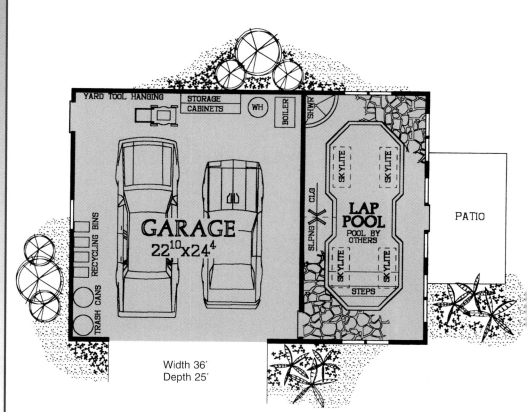

YARD TOOL HANGING · STORAGE CABINETS · WH · BOILER · SHWR

RECYCLING BINS

TRASH CANS

GARAGE
22^{10}x24^4

SLPNG · CLG

SKYLITE · SKYLITE

LAP POOL
POOL BY OTHERS

SKYLITE · SKYLITE

STEPS

PATIO

Width 36'
Depth 25'

Plan G270

Plan G271

Plan G273

The Dog House

PLAN G266

▶ Not a hideout for an errant spouse, this floor plan is a two-car garage, plus seven-pen kennel. Looking like a guest cottage from the outside, the area adjacent to the garage holds seven 4' x 5'-6" dog pens. A grooming area with deep sink and storage cabinets is in the rear near the back door which opens onto the dog run. A 16' x 7' door provides access to the garage for cars. Extra storage for yard and garden equipment as well as recycling and trash bins is also provided.

Choose The Quartermain (Plan G268), The Fox Hunt (Plan G267), or The Greyhound (G269) for a different look. Design by Home Planners

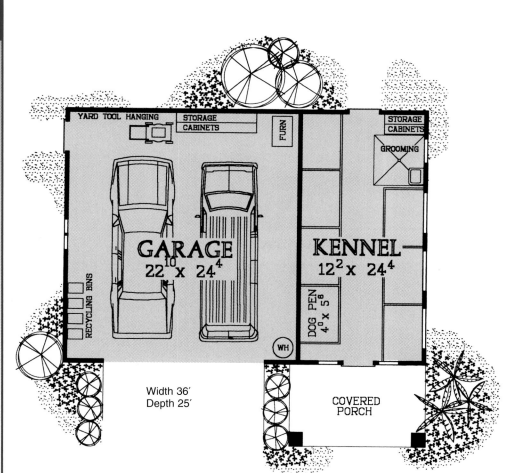

Width 36′
Depth 25′

Plan G269

Plan G267

Plan G268

E. REINKE

Now And Then

BASIC PLAN

PLAN G300

▶ Start small with this elegant, 17' x 17', free-standing garden room. Use the space as a garden retreat for reading or music, or as an arts-and-crafts studio. Two tall, arched windows topped with fanlights grace three sides. A window and entry door flanked by narrow mock shutters are found in the front. The vented cupola and weathervane centered on the cedar shake roof add an air of rustic charm. To expand on a good thing, extend the floor plan to each side. Add an entry foyer and full bath to one side of the existing structure and a breakfast nook with its own door to the garden on the other. Existing windows become doorways and, in one case, a window is replaced by an interior wall. To complete this outstanding expansion, add an 11' x 15' bedroom with generous closets off the foyer, and an 11' x 10'-10" kitchen with pass-through window off the breakfast nook. Behind the kitchen is space for more storage or a mini-workshop. Design by Home Planners

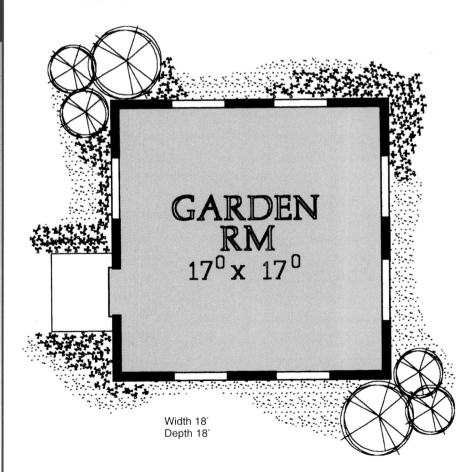

GARDEN RM
17^0 x 17^0

Width 18'
Depth 18'

EXPANDED PLAN

SLPNG X CLG

BATH   SHWR

BEDRM
11⁰ x 15⁰

FOYER

LIVING
RM
17⁰ x 17⁰

NOOK
10² x 13⁰

MECH /
STORAGE

REF   BC

PASS-THRU

KIT
11⁰ x10¹⁰

S

SLPNG X CLG   RANGE

Width 62′
Depth 18′

COTTAGES AND STUDIOS

Work And Play

PLAN G109

▶ Sunshine and fresh air pour into every inch of this functional garden cottage through the arched roofline above the support columns and the fanlights above the French doors and tall double-hung windows. Grab some rays outside on the deck, or inside in the bright and cheerful sunroom. Work, if you must, at a built-in table with an ample counter stretching out on either side. This is the perfect place to spread out all the pieces of a sewing or craft project, or that never-ending report that requires graphs and charts and maximum organization. Design by Home Planners

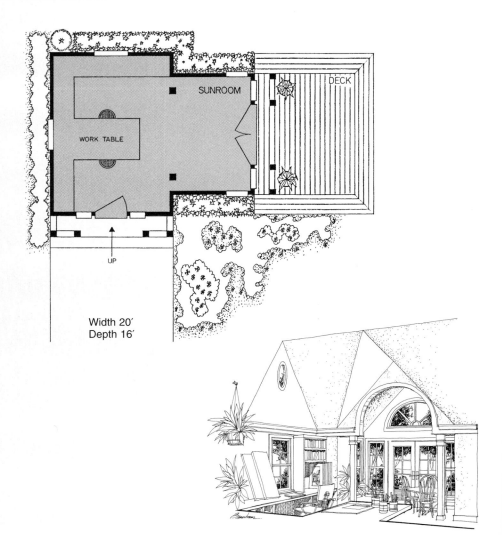

Width 20´
Depth 16´

Town and Country

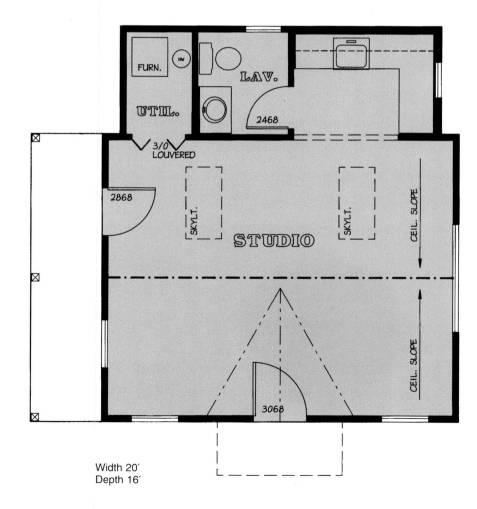

Width 20'
Depth 16'

FURN.   HW

UTIL.

LAV.

3/0 LOUVERED

2868

SKYLT.

SKYLT.

STUDIO

CEIL. SLOPE

CEIL. SLOPE

2468

3068

PLAN G230

▶ This versatile design features a unique siding pattern: a little bit of country with a pinch of contemporary sophistication. You can build this 320-square-foot, multi-purpose structure on a slab or crawlspace or even with a basement! Planned to take advantage of natural light from all sides, this design will make a perfect studio, game room or office. Or, add a shower in the lavatory room and it becomes a guest house. Features include a half bath, a 6' x 18' kitchen—large enough for a stove and refrigerator—and a utility room with ample space for a furnace and hot water tank. With all the amenities provided, you could work or relax here for days without ever leaving! The front porch area is a charming place to relax and put your feet up as you or your guests contemplate the events of the day. Design by Home Planners.

Country Cottage

PLAN 9133

▶ A lot of living can be packed into this cozy Victorian cottage with a 440-square-foot apartment on the first floor and an additional 126 square feet available in the loft above. The 10' x 10'-8" bedroom and 11' x 15' living room provide plenty of space for one person or a couple. A full bath and kitchenette provide the necessities. A charming dining nook in a sunny bow window and a spiral staircase up to the loft add special touches. It's the perfect answer for keeping watch over aging parents or for use as a home office or weekend guest cottage. Design by Larry W. Garnett and Associates, Inc.

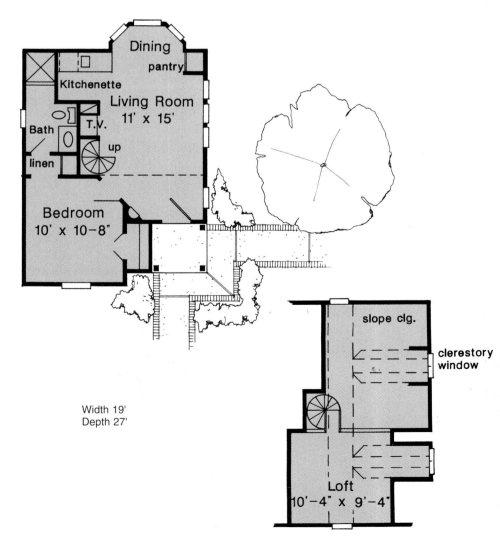

Width 19'
Depth 27'

Gate House

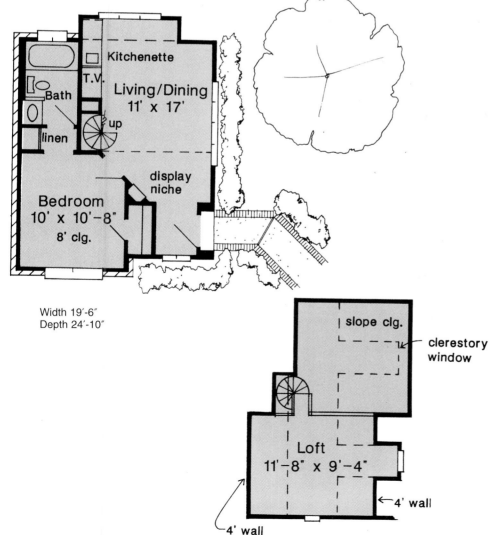

Kitchenette

T.V.

Living/Dining
11' x 17'

Bath

linen

up

display
niche

Bedroom
10' x 10'–8"
8' clg.

Width 19'-6"
Depth 24'-10"

slope clg.

clerestory
window

Loft
11'–8" x 9'–4"

4' wall

4' wall

PLAN 9132

▶ This enchanting cottage is reminiscent of the guest quarters and gate houses of English country estates. Convert it to your own requirements with or without an optional 132-square-foot loft. The 10' x 10'-8" bedroom and large living/dining area, plus full bath and kitchenette, make this ideal for weekend guests or a quiet environment for your home office. Replace the shingle siding shown with stucco or horizontal siding to make this versatile design compatible with your main house. Design by Larry W. Garnett and Associates, Inc.

Fieldstone

PLAN 9094

▶ Enter this charming cottage through a covered porch with fieldstone walls. The design makes the most of the 627-square-foot, first-floor living area and provides additional space with a 90-square-foot optional loft. French Doors on the 12' x 12' bedroom, a bow window in the kitchen, and a vaulted ceiling with a clerestory dormer window bring the outdoors in. An incline ladder reaches the loft in this ideal getaway retreat. Design by Larry W. Garnett and Associates, Inc.

Br
12' x 12'

incline ladder

Kit

Living
13' x 15'

Dining

Width 24'
Depth 36'-4"

Loft

Living Below
vaulted ceiling

8' x 9'

clerestory window

Cross Breeze

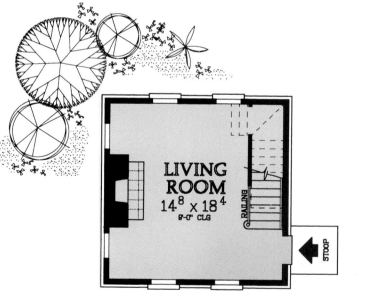

LIVING
ROOM
14^8 x 18^4
9'-0" CLG

RAILING

STOOP

Width 20'
Depth 20'

▶ Capture elusive breezes upstairs or down through the matching sets of windows in this stately two-story guest house or office suite. In the winter months, allow only sun in through the windows and enjoy the warmth and charm of a fireplace on both floors. A generous 14'- 8" x 18'- 4" square-foot living area occupies the entire first floor. Upstairs you'll be at home—or at work—in a 14'- 8 " x 12' -6" bedroom/office area, plus a bath with a shower. Design by Home Planners

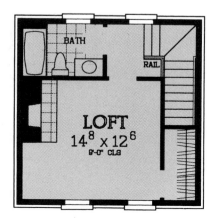

BATH

RAIL

LOFT
14^8 x 12^6
9'-0" CLG

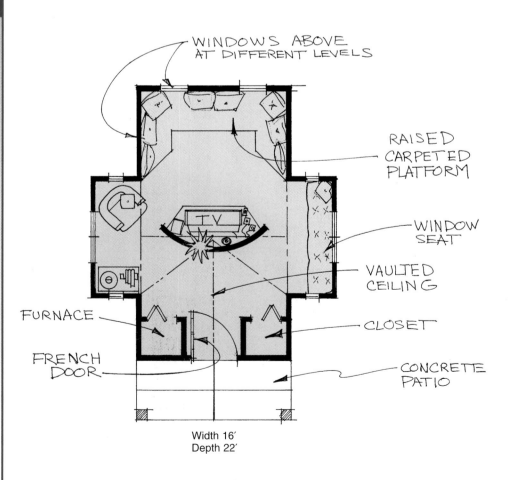

Playhouse

PLAN R126

▶ Lucky are the kids who visit this whimsical "kids kottage." The colorful exterior includes playful shapes and turned windows which—with a little imagination—make a face with eyes, nose, mouth, and eyebrows! A French door off the sheltered patio opens on a brightly painted "graffiti" wall which wraps around a built-in TV seating area. A raised and carpeted seating platform and built-in window seat, plus specially designed games center, provide lots of options for fun. Design by Home Planners

WINDOWS ABOVE AT DIFFERENT LEVELS

RAISED CARPETED PLATFORM

WINDOW SEAT

VAULTED CEILING

CLOSET

CONCRETE PATIO

FURNACE

FRENCH DOOR

Width 16'
Depth 22'

The Get-Away

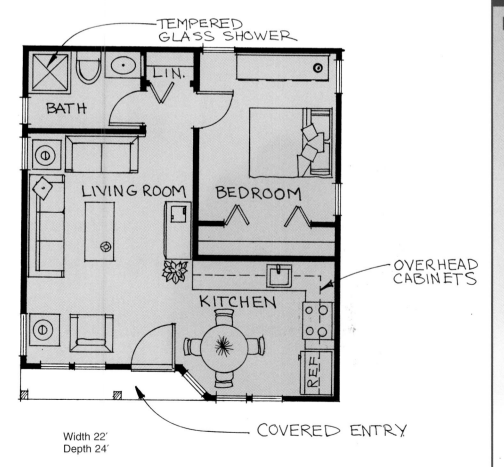

TEMPERED
GLASS SHOWER

LIN.

BATH

LIVING ROOM

BEDROOM

OVERHEAD
CABINETS

KITCHEN

REF.

COVERED ENTRY

Width 22′
Depth 24′

PLAN R130

▶ A wide porch graces the entry to this cottage plan, providing a compact, but fully functional apartment. Mill-turned columns support the roof overhang and the front door opens into the generous living room. A kitchen nook has room for a table and chairs and plenty of overhead cabinets. More storage is available in the bedroom—a large closet with folding doors. A full bath with a tempered glass shower and a linen closet in the hall make this a perfect apartment for an elderly parent or a not-quite-ready-to-leave-home teen. Design by Home Planners

Big Kid's Playhouse

PLAN G228

▶ This large, 80-square-foot Victorian playhouse is for the kid in all of us. With enough space to hold bunk beds, use it for overnight adventures. Young children will spend hours playing in this little house. Older kids will find it a haven for quiet study or a perfect private retreat. Four windows flood the interior with natural light, and a single-door entrance provides access from the porch. The 8'-1" overall height will accommodate most adults and the addition of electricity and water would expand the versatility of this unit. Designed on a concrete slab, this playhouse could be placed on a wooden frame for future relocation or change in function after the kids leave home. Design by Home Planners

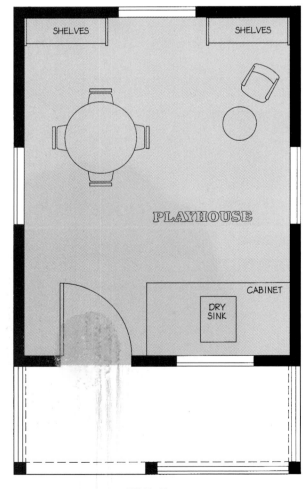

Width 8'
Depth 13'

STORAGE AND GARDEN SHEDS

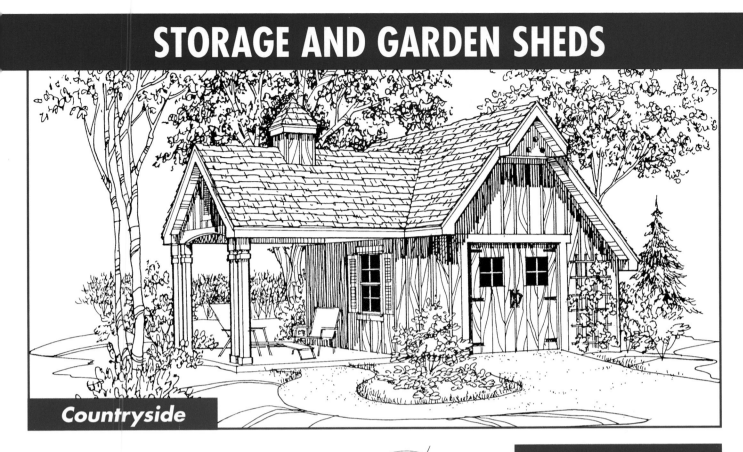

Countryside

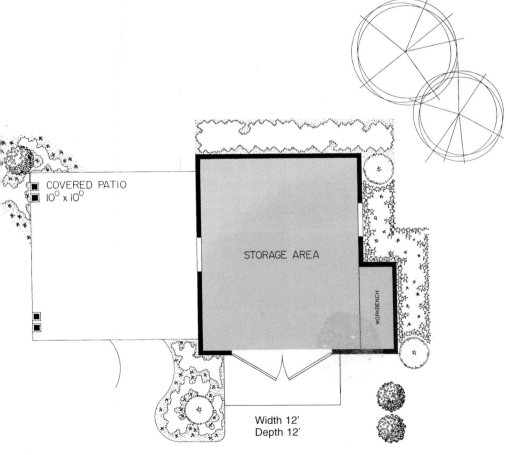

COVERED PATIO
10⁰ x 10⁰

STORAGE AREA

WORKBENCH

Width 12'
Depth 12'

PLAN G107

▶ Hinged, double doors open onto a generous 12' x 12' storage area for yard and garden equipment or off-season sporting gear. A built-in workbench along the side wall allows for handy repairs or a potting bench. Windows in each side wall bring in natural light and plenty of fresh air. But to catch the real breeze, try the 10' x 10' covered patio with four mill-turned support columns and a gently arched roofline. Add a shingled cupola just for fun, and tuck a birdhouse in the eves. Design by Home Planners

STORAGE AND GARDEN SHEDS

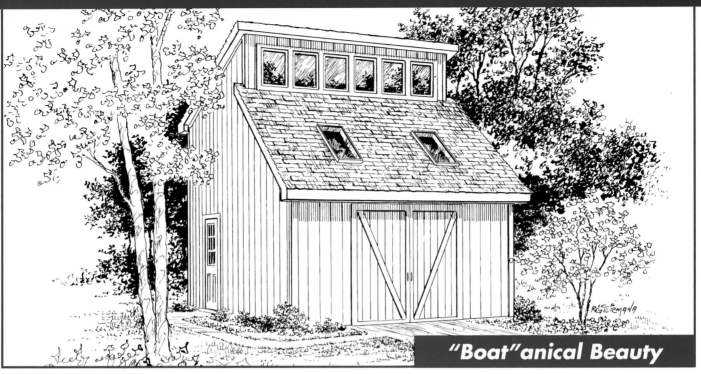

"Boat"anical Beauty

PLAN G223

▶ This large multi-level garden shed can be easily modified to become a boat house if yours is a nautical family. As a lawn or garden shed, there is ample room for all your garden equipment, with a separate area for potting plants. The built-in potting bench features removable planks to accommodate flats of flowers in various sizes. The roomy loft provides 133 square feet of safe storage area for chemicals, fertilizers or other lawn-care products. Natural light floods the interior through multiple windows in the rear wall and in the front, across from the storage loft. This practical structure can also be used as a studio or, placed at the water's edge, it can be easily converted to a boat house by adding 4' x 4' columns used as piers in lieu of the slab floor. Design by Home Planners

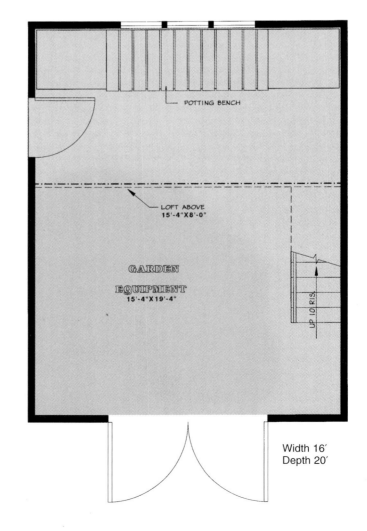

POTTING BENCH

LOFT ABOVE
15'-4"X8'-0"

GARDEN
EQUIPMENT
15'-4"X19'-4"

UP 10 RIS.

Width 16'
Depth 20'

Work And/Or Play

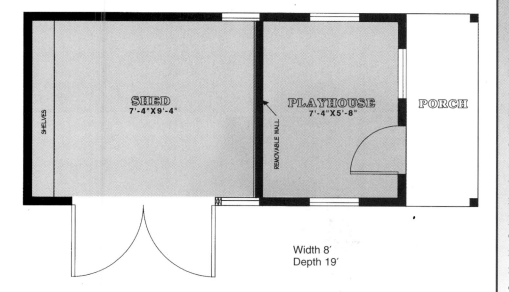

SHELVES

SHED
7'-4"X 9'-4"

REMOVABLE WALL

PLAYHOUSE
7'-4"X 5'-8"

PORCH

Width 8'
Depth 19'

PLAN G227

▶ This functional, practical lawn shed doubles in design and capacity as a delightful playhouse complete with a covered porch, lathe-turned columns and a window box for young gardeners. The higher roofline on the shed gives the structure a two-story effect, while the playhouse design gives the simple lawn shed a much more appealing appearance. The shed is accessed through double doors. The playhouse features a single-door entrance from the porch and three bright windows. The interior wall between the shed and playhouse could be moved another two-and-a-half feet back to make it larger. Or remove the interior wall completely to use the entire 128-square-foot area exclusively for either the lawn shed or playhouse. Design by Home Planners

Two-Door Tudor

PLAN G225

▶ Lawn-shed extraordinaire, this appealing design can be easily converted from the Tudor style shown here to match just about any exterior design you prefer. In addition to serving as a lawn shed, this versatile structure also can be used as a craft studio, a pool house or a delightful play-house for your children. The double doors and large floor area provide ample access and storage capacity for lawn tractors and other large pieces of equipment. A handy built-in work bench offers needed space for potting plants or working on craft projects. A separate storage room for craft supplies, lawn-care products or pool chemicals can be locked for safety. Strategically placed on your site, this charming building could be designed to be a reflection of your home in miniature. Design by Home Planners

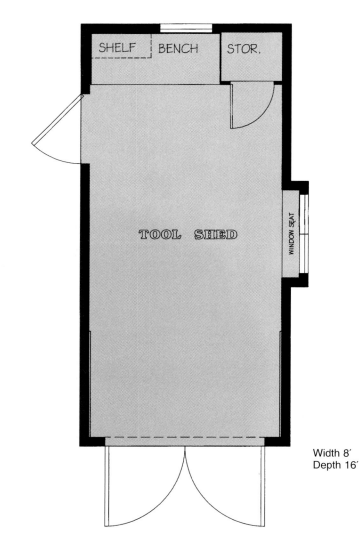

Width 8′
Depth 16′

Double Duty

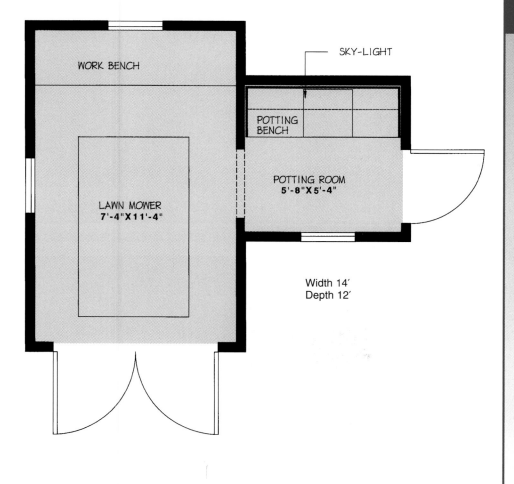

WORK BENCH

SKY-LIGHT

POTTING
BENCH

LAWN MOWER
7'-4"X 11'-4"

POTTING ROOM
5'-8"X 5'-4"

Width 14'
Depth 12'

PLAN G222

▶ Open the double doors of this multi-purpose structure and it's a mini-garage for tools. Enter by the single door, and it's a potting shed complete with potting bench and skylight. The tool-shed section is large enough—7'-4" x 11'-4"—to house the largest lawn tractor, with room to spare for other garden equipment such as shovels, rakes, lawn trimmers and hoses. With windows on all sides and a skylight above the potting bench, the interior has plenty of natural light —the addition of electrical wiring would make this structure even more practical. The design is shown in a Victorian style, but a different appearance can be accomplished by modifying the trim, windows and siding to match any gable-roof home design. Design by Home Planners

STORAGE AND GARDEN SHEDS

Change-Up

PLAN G224

▶ Here's a unique design that can be converted to serve a variety of functions: a tool shed, a barbecue stand, a pool-supply depot or a sports equipment locker. Apply a little "what-if" imagination to come up with additional ways to use this versatile design to enhance your outdoor living space. As a tool shed, this design features a large potting bench with storage above and below. Second, as a summer kitchen, it includes a built-in grill, a sink and a refrigerator. Third, for use as a pool-supply depot or equipment storage, it comes with a locker to store chemicals or valuable sports equipment safely. This structure is designed to be movable but, depending on its function, could be placed on a concrete slab. Design by Home Planners

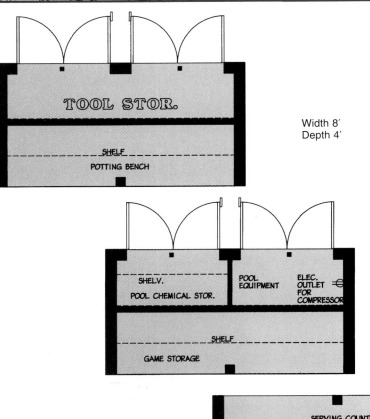

TOOL STOR.

SHELF

POTTING BENCH

Width 8′
Depth 4′

SHELV.

POOL CHEMICAL STOR.

POOL EQUIPMENT

ELEC. OUTLET FOR COMPRESSOR

SHELF

GAME STORAGE

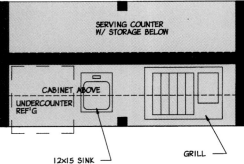

SERVING COUNTER W/ STORAGE BELOW

CABINET ABOVE

UNDERCOUNTER REF'G

12x15 SINK

GRILL

Little House In The Garden

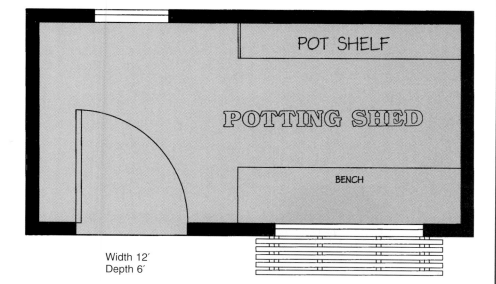

POT SHELF

POTTING SHED

BENCH

Width 12'
Depth 6'

PLAN G247

▶ Designed to accent its surroundings, this cozy little building keeps all your garden tools and supplies at your fingertips. You can vary the materials to create the appearance best suited to your site. This 12' x 6' structure is large enough to accommodate a potting bench, shelves and an area for garden tools. The window above the potting bench allows ample light, but electricity could be added easily. Designed to be built on a concrete slab, you could use treated lumber for the floor joists, and sit it right on the ground. To convert this shed design to a playhouse, simply change the window shelf into a planter and add a step with a handrail at the door. Design by Home Planners.

BARNS AND STABLES

Rural Hideaway

PLAN G226

▶ This large, sturdy lawn shed is not quite "as big as a barn," but almost! A combined area of 768 square feet includes a 24' x 16' loft area with access by ladder or stairway. The structure is built entirely of standard framing materials requiring no special beams or cutting. An ideal hideaway for the serious artist, this structure could serve a myriad of other uses including a second garage, a game house, or even as a barn for small livestock. Or, with a little imagination this could be converted by your contractor to be a secluded guest house. The large tool room at the back has a built-in work bench with plenty of natural light, plus entrances from inside or outside. A 6' x 7' sliding-door entrance with crossbars, and a louvered cupola, accent the rural effect. Design by Home Planners.

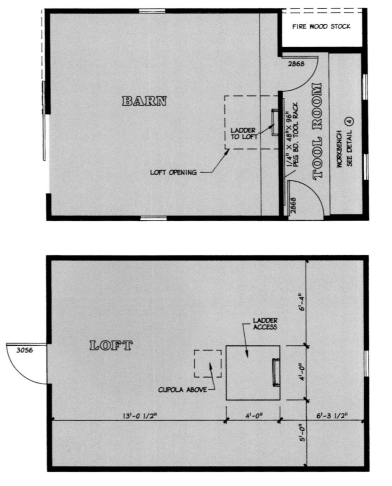

Width 24'
Depth 16'

The Derby

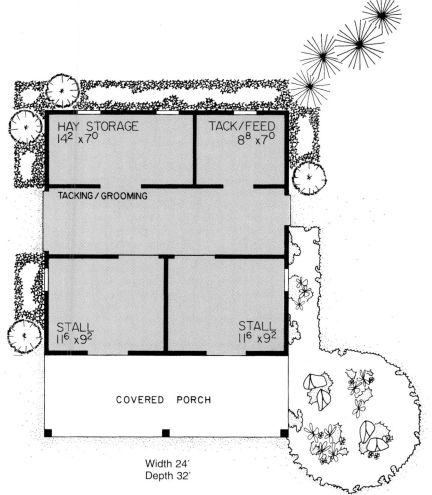

HAY STORAGE
14^2 x 7^0

TACK/FEED
8^8 x 7^0

TACKING / GROOMING

STALL
11^6 x 9^2

STALL
11^6 x 9^2

COVERED PORCH

Width 24'
Depth 32'

PLAN G113

▶ Right out of Kentucky horse country comes this all-in-one design for a two-horse stable, plus tack room and covered hay storage. Two generous 11'-6" x 9'-2" stalls provide shelter and security for your best stock, with easy access through Dutch doors. Against the far wall is a 14'-2" x 7' hay "loft" and next to it, an 8'-8" x 7' tack room. In the center is a large area reserved for grooming your mount or to saddle up for the big race. Design by Home Planners

BARNS AND STABLES

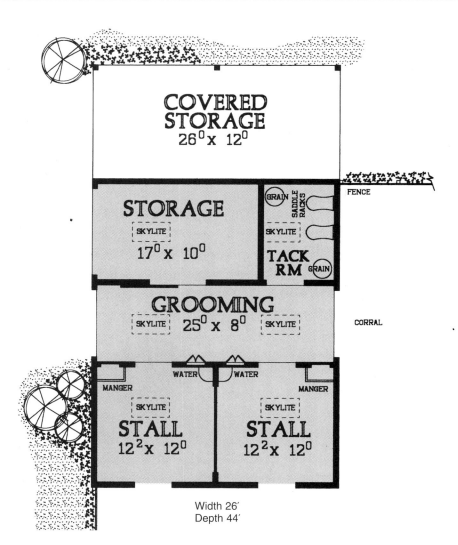

Horse Country

PLAN G291

▶ With 1,144 square feet under roof, this expanded structure will be home to your prize stock. Outside, a 26' x 12' covered area with a concrete floor provides storage and parking for tractors and other equipment. Inside, six skylights illuminate the interior of three major areas: 1) two 12'-2" x 12' pens with dirt floors, each with built-in feed troughs, fresh-water hook ups, and Dutch doors leading to an outdoor fenced area; 2) a covered grooming area with sloped, grooved concrete flooring and maximum access through double doors at each end; and 3) a 17' x 10' storage area with concrete floors for hay and a 7'-6" x 10' secured tack room with built-in saddle racks. Design by Home Planners

COVERED STORAGE 26⁰ x 12⁰

FENCE

STORAGE SKYLITE 17⁰ x 10⁰

GRAIN · SADDLE RACKS

SKYLITE

TACK RM GRAIN

GROOMING SKYLITE 25⁰ x 8⁰ SKYLITE

CORRAL

WATER WATER

MANGER MANGER

SKYLITE **STALL** 12²x 12⁰

SKYLITE **STALL** 12²x 12⁰

Width 26'
Depth 44'

4-H Plus

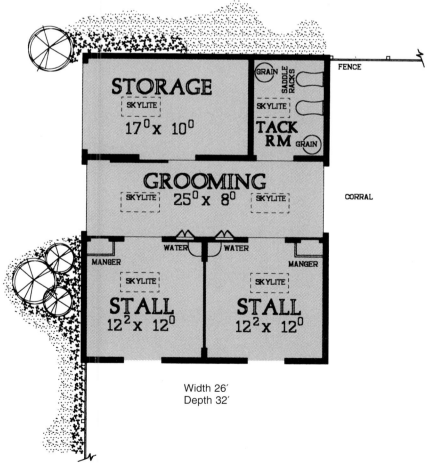

STORAGE
SKYLITE
17⁰ x 10⁰

GRAIN
SADDLE RACKS
SKYLITE
TACK RM
GRAIN

FENCE

GROOMING
SKYLITE 25⁰ x 8⁰ SKYLITE

CORRAL

WATER WATER

MANGER
SKYLITE
STALL
12²x 12⁰

MANGER
SKYLITE
STALL
12²x 12⁰

Width 26′
Depth 32′

PLAN G290

▶ Tailor this floor plan to meet your needs or your youngster's 4H project. With the same building dimensions as Plan G291, this plan is minus the roof extension and the concrete patio area to be added at a later time or to accommodate a smaller area. Add a whimsical cupola if you choose, but the same functional capacity remains inside with storage for hay and tack, a generous grooming area with concrete floor, and skylights to provide natural light. Large 12'-2" x 12' livestock pens have dirt floors and built-in feed and water facilities. Design by Home Planners

El Grande

PLAN G292

▶ If you run a large operation, consider this expanded floor plan for your stable requirements. Six 12'-2" x 12' livestock pens with dirt floors feature built-in feed and water troughs and Dutch doors leading either to a fenced exercise area or into either of two conveniently located grooming areas. Both grooming areas have grooved cement floors, sloped for easy hosing and draining. A convenient connecting hall between the grooming areas also has sloped concrete floors for easy maintenance. A central secured tack room with built-in saddle racks and grain bins, a bath with a toilet and a sink, and a 10' x 17' inside storage area for hay complete the available features. Seven skylights throughout the structure provide an abundance of natural light. Design by Home Planners

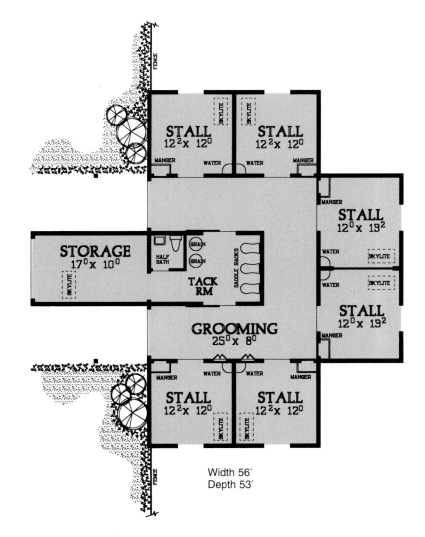

Width 56'
Depth 53'

CABANAS AND PAVILIONS

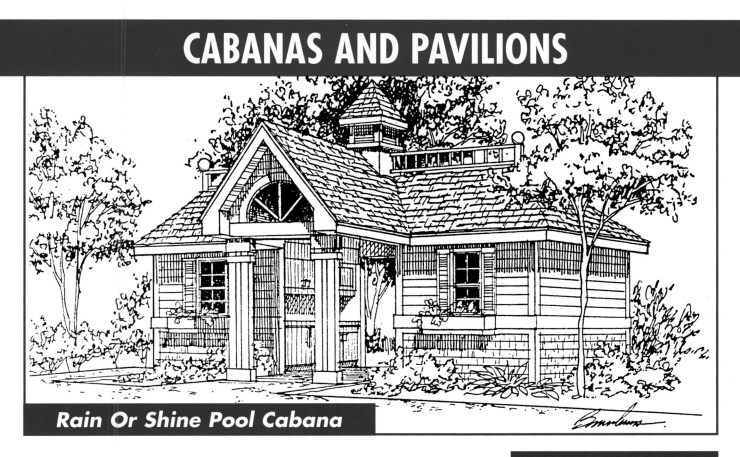

Rain Or Shine Pool Cabana

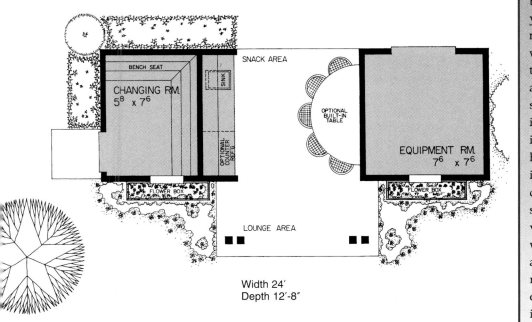

BENCH SEAT

CHANGING RM.
5⁸ x 7⁶

SINK

SNACK AREA

OPTIONAL
COUNTER
REF G

OPTIONAL
BUILT-IN
TABLE

EQUIPMENT RM.
7⁶ x 7⁶

FLOWER BOX

FLOWER BOX

LOUNGE AREA

Width 24'
Depth 12'-8"

PLAN G110

▶ A mini-kitchen and an optional built-in table are tucked in the breezeway of this double room; you'll have shelter for poolside repasts no matter what the weather. You can enhance both the beauty and the function of any pool area with this charming structure. The exterior features include a gable roof with columns in the front, shuttered windows, horizontal wood and shingle siding, decorative flower boxes and a cupola. The two rooms on either side of the breezeway area provide a 5'-8" x 7'-6" changing area with built-in seating and a larger area—7'-6" x 7'-6"—for convenient storage for pool supplies and equipment. This spacious cabana is sure to be a fine addition to an active family's pool area. Design by Home Planners

CABANAS AND PAVILIONS

Triple Duty

PLAN G239

▶ A changing room, a summer kitchen, and an elegant porch for shade—all in one! Add the convenience of bathroom facilities and you're set for outdoor living all summer long. This pool pavilion is designed to provide maximum function in a small area and features built-in benches, shelves, hanging rods and a separate linen closet for towels. The opaque diamond-patterned windows decorate the exterior of the 9'-4" x 6' changing area and the mirror-image bath. The bath could also be made into a kitchen area, then simply add a sliding window to allow easy passage of refreshments to your family and guests at poolside. When you've had enough sun or socializing, recline in the shade under the columned porch and enjoy a good book or a nap. Design by Home Planners

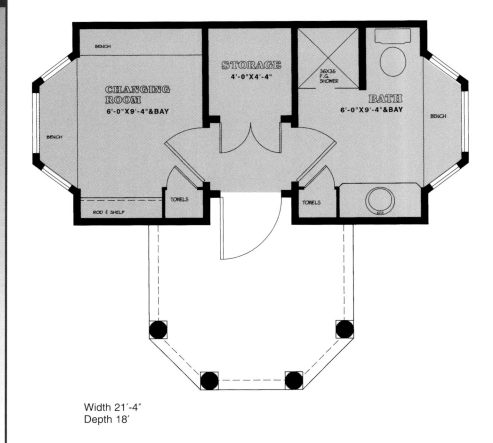

Width 21'-4"
Depth 18'

Quick-Change Architecture

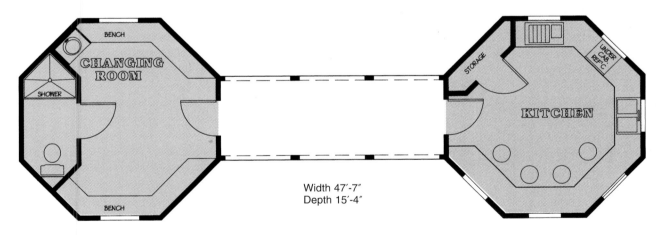

BENCH

CHANGING ROOM

SHOWER

BENCH

STORAGE

UNDER CAB. REF. C.

KITCHEN

Width 47'-7"
Depth 15'-4"

PLAN G238

▶The magic of this design is its flexibility. Use it exclusively as a changing cabana with separate His and Hers changing rooms, or, with a little sleight of hand, turn one of the rooms into a summer kitchen for outdoor entertaining. As changing rooms, the two eight-sided areas include built-in benches and private bathroom facilities. The 15'-3.5" x 15'-3.5" kitchen option includes a stove, refrigerator, food preparation area and storage pantry. A shuttered window poolside provides easy access to serve your guests across the counter. Linking these two areas is a covered walkway which serves as a shaded picnic area, or a convenient place to get out of the sun. Columns, arches and stained-glass windows provide a touch of grandeur to this fun and functional poolside design. Design by Home Planners

Four Corners

PLAN G293

▶ Look at all you can get into this 24' x 24' inside-outside area at poolside! Four corner units are united by open-air walkways and are almost literally tied together by a trellis roof. Pull up a chair to the outside snack bar in one corner for a refreshing drink or snack. Across the walkway is an efficiency kitchenette to make the goodies. In the next corner is a restroom and a shower, each with a separate entrance. The final corner hides all the pool essentials with double doors leading to the filter and pump room and a separate storage room for other pool equipment and toys. Design by Home Planners

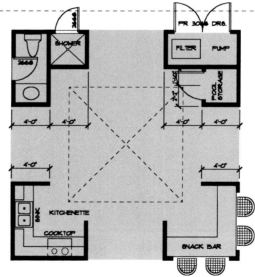

Width 24'
Depth 24'

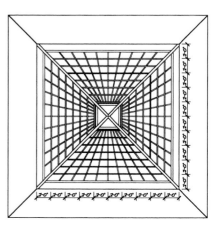

ROOF PLAN

Exercise Escape

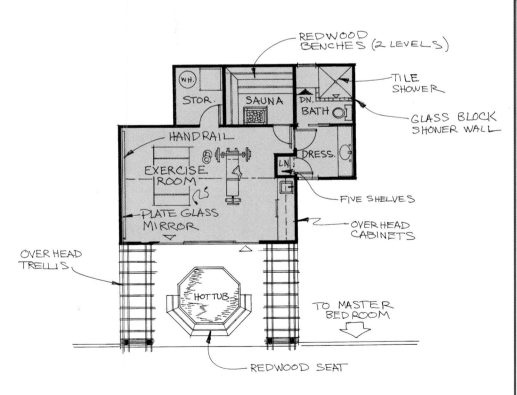

REDWOOD BENCHES (2 LEVELS)

TILE SHOWER

GLASS BLOCK SHOWER WALL

W.H.

STOR.

SAUNA

DN.

BATH

HANDRAIL

EXERCISE ROOM

DRESS.

L.N.

FIVE SHELVES

PLATE GLASS MIRROR

OVER HEAD CABINETS

OVER HEAD TRELLIS

HOT TUB

TO MASTER BEDROOM

REDWOOD SEAT

Width 28'
Depth 21'

PLAN R129

▶ This simple gable-roofed exercise cottage blends with many house styles. Trellises visually link the cottage and the main house; they also provide a sense of privacy and an enclosure for the hot tub. The main exercise room provides more than 250 square feet of floor space and more than 12 feet of head room to house the most serious equipment. Mirrors and a ballet bar line one wall. The mini-kitchen features a sink and a refrigerator. Doors lead to bathroom and sauna. Vaulted ceilings and double-decked windows give a bright, inviting feeling. Design by Home Planners

Designer Playhouse

PLAN G114

▶ This whimsical, scaled-down version of a full-size house makes a dream-come-true playhouse for kids. Designed by Conni Cross, it features a wraparound front porch with a trellis roof, a "real" front door and a loft that can only be reached by a ladder through a trap door! Generous dimensions provide plenty of space for a 7'-4" x 9'-4" play room and a 5'-8" x 6'-4" bunk room. A 7'-4" x 5'-4" loft overlooks the main play area. Natural light floods all areas of this delightful play center through windows in the play room, bunk room and loft. A sturdy railing borders the loft, and built-in bunk beds in the bunk room are ready and waiting for sleep-overs. Design by Home Planners

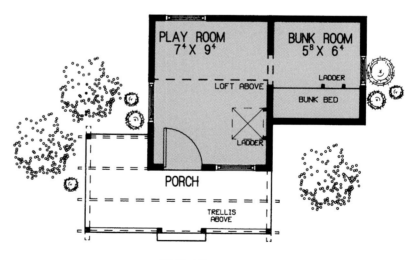

Width 18'
Depth 14'

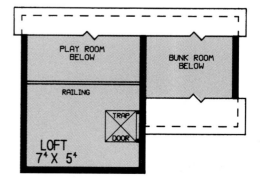

Y'all Come!

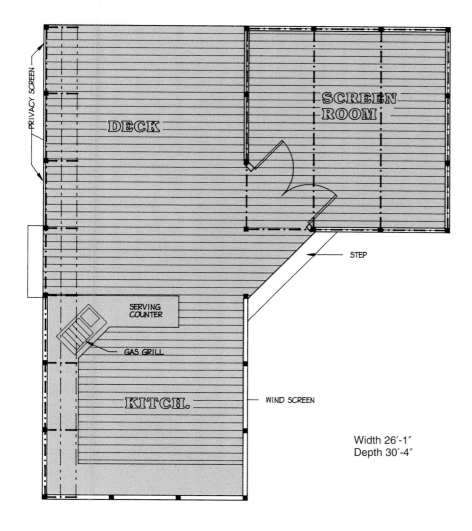

PRIVACY SCREEN

DECK

SCREEN ROOM

STEP

SERVING COUNTER

GAS GRILL

KITCH.

WIND SCREEN

Width 26'-1"
Depth 30'-4"

▶An outdoor kitchen and much, much more! For year-round, daylight-to-dark entertaining, consider this large outdoor entertainment unit. Nearly 700 square feet of floor space includes a deck for sunbathing by day or dancing under the stars after sundown. A 13' x 13'-2" screened room provides a pest-free environment for cards or conversation. And the Cookout Chef will rule with a flair over a full-service kitchen area that may include a grill, wet bar, sink, refrigerator and ample room for storage. You can locate this versatile structure adjacent to your pool, or place it as a free-standing unit wherever your landscape and site plan allow. Select material for the railings and privacy screens in patterns to match or complement your home. Design by Home Planners

Country Garden

PLAN G221

▶ The built-in planters and open roof areas of this multiple-entrance gazebo make this design a gardener's dream-come-true. The open roof allows sun and rain ample access to the planters and gives the structure a definite country-garden effect. Built with or without a cupola, the open-air lattice work in the walls and roof complements a wide variety of landscapes and home designs. A creative gardener will soon enhance this charming gazebo with a wealth of plants and vines. Tuck a birdbath or bubbling fountain into a corner to further the garden setting. The large design—256 square feet—ensures that both you and nature have plenty of room to share all that this gazebo has to offer. It easily accommodates a table and chairs when you invite your guests to this outdoor hide-away. Design by Home Planners

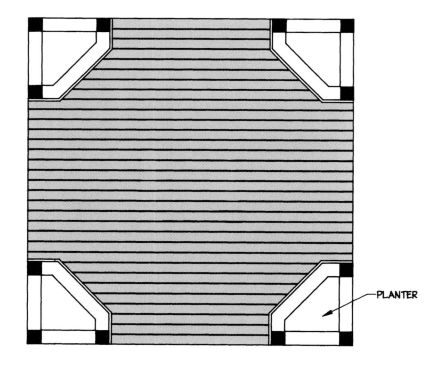

PLANTER

Width 16'
Depth 16'

Kaleidoscope

PLAN G219

▶ Shining copper on the cupola and shimmering glass windows all around enhance this double-entrance gazebo with dancing light and color. The many windows allow natural light to engulf the interior, making it a perfect studio. Easy to heat and cool, this gazebo contains operable louvers in the cupola to increase the flow of air. An exhaust fan could be added to the cupola to further maximize air flow. The masonry base with brick steps gives the structure a definite feeling of both elegance and permanence. The roof structure is made from standard framing materials with the cupola adorned with a copper cover. If cost is a factor, the cupola roof could be made of asphalt shingles and the glass windows could be eliminated. Design by Home Planners

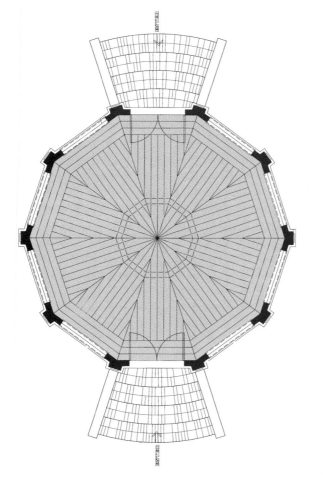

Width 19'-10"
Depth 29'-6"

BLUEPRINT PACKAGE

For Garages, Sheds & Outdoor Buildings

The blueprint package for these inspiring structures contains everything you need to plan and build the outdoor amenity of your choice. Some of the more complicated plans packages will have several sheets to thoroughly explain how the structure will go together. The simpler structures such as sheds and gazebos have fewer sheets.

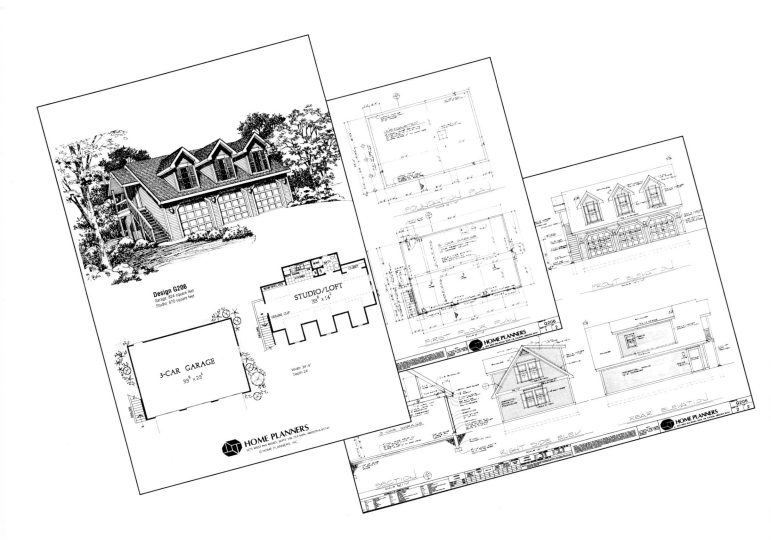

The plans for our structures have been custom-created by a professional designer. Among the helpful sheets for building your structure may be such information as:

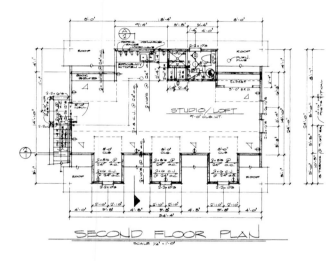

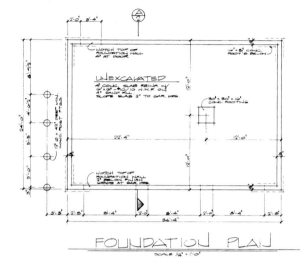

Floor Plan

Drawn in convenient scale, this sheet shows the exact floor plan of the structure with dimensions, flooring patterns and window and door call-outs. Details found on other sheets may also be referenced on this sheet.

Foundation and Joist Details/Materials List

This schematic of the foundation and floor and rafter joists, drawn in convenient scale, gives dimensions and shows how to pour or construct the foundation and flooring components. The materials list is invaluable for estimating and planning work and acts as an accurate "shopping list" for the do-it-yourselfer.

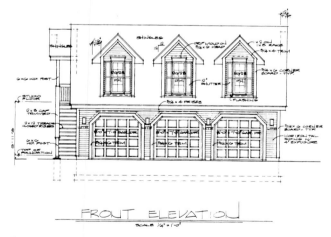

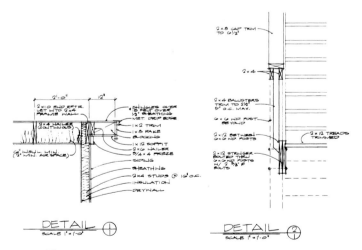

Elevations and Framing Plans/Wall Sections

Drawn in convenient scale, these helpful drawings show various views of the structure plus a complete framing plan for the flooring. Wall sections provide stud sizes, connector types, and rafter and roofing materials. They may also show mouldings or other trim pieces.

Details

Cut-out details, drawn in convenient scale, are given for items such as pilaster framing, doors, side panels and rafter profiles. These details provide additional information and enhance your understanding of other aspects of the plans.

TO ORDER, CALL TOLL FREE 1-800-521-6797

PRICE INDEX

For Garages & Other Outdoor Structures

Blueprint Price Schedule
(Prices guaranteed through December 31, 1999)

Price Group	GD1	GD2	GD3	GD4	GD5	GD6
1 set Custom Plans	$20	$40	$50	$60	$75	$85

Additional Identical Sets......................................$10
Reverse Sets (mirror image) $10

Plan	Page	Price	Plan	Page	Price	Plan	Page	Price
7000	40	GD5	G201A	41	GD6	G272	56	GD4
8901	43	GD6	G206	32	GD6	G273	57	GD4
8920	38	GD5	G219	91	GD2	G274	53	GD4
8921	39	GD5	G221	90	GD2	G275	53	GD4
8972	17	GD3	G222	75	GD2	G276	53	GD4
8974	16	GD3	G223	72	GD2	G277	52	GD4
8977	26	GD3	G224	76	GD1	G278	51	GD4
8978	42	GD6	G225	74	GD2	G279	50	GD4
8988	34	GD6	G226	78	GD3	G280	51	GD4
9094	66	$250	G227	73	GD2	G281	51	GD4
9132	65	$250	G228	70	GD2	G282	45	GD4
9133	64	$250	G230	63	GD3	G283	45	GD4
9193	35	GD5	G238	85	GD3	G284	45	GD4
G100	46	GD4	G239	84	GD3	G285	44	GD4
G101	24	GD3	G241	89	GD5	G286	31	GD4
G102	20	GD3	G247	77	GD1	G287	31	GD5
G103	28	GD2	G254	13	GD3	G288	31	GD5
G104	14	GD3	G255	12	GD3	G289	30	GD5
G105	22	GD3	G256	13	GD3	G290	81	GD5
G106	36	GD5	G257	13	GD3	G291	80	GD5
G107	71	GD3	G258	55	GD4	G292	82	GD6
G109	62	GD3	G259	54	GD4	G293	86	GD4
G110	83	GD3	G260	55	GD4	G294	19	GD3
G111	47	GD4	G261	55	GD4	G295	19	GD3
G113	79	GD4	G262	49	GD4	G296	19	GD3
G114	88	GD2	G263	49	GD4	G297	18	GD3
G116	29	GD2	G264	49	GD4	G300	60	$250
G117	29	GD2	G265	48	GD4	G301	67	$250
G118	25	GD3	G266	58	GD4	G302	33	GD6
G119	23	GD3	G267	59	GD4	R126	68	GD5
G122	27	GD3	G268	59	GD4	R128	37	GD6
G123	15	GD3	G269	59	GD4	R129	87	GD6
G125	21	GD3	G270	57	GD4	R130	69	GD6
G201	11	GD6	G271	57	GD4			

BLUEPRINT ORDER FORM
For Garages & Other Outdoor Structures

TO ORDER: Find the Plan number in the Plans Index (opposite). Consult the Price Schedule (opposite) to determine the price of your plan, adding any additional or reverse sets you desire. Complete the order form on this page and mail with your check or money order. Please include the correct postage and handling fees. If you prefer, you can also use a credit card and call our toll-free number, 1-800-521-6797, to place your order.

Our Service Policy
We try to process and ship every order from our office within two business days. For this reason, we won't send a formal notice acknowledging receipt of your order.

Our Exchange Policy
Because we produce and ship plans in response to individual orders, we cannot honor requests for refunds. However, you can exchange your entire order of blueprints, including a single set if you order just one, for a set of another design. All exchanges carry an additional fee of $15.00 plus $15.00 postage and handling if they're sent Regular Service; $20.00 via Priority; $30.00 via Express.

About Reverse Blueprints
If you want to install your structure in reverse of the plan as shown, we will include an extra set of blueprints with the images reversed for an additional fee of $10.00. Although callouts and lettering appear backward, reverses will prove useful as a visual aid if you decide to flop the plan.

How Many Blueprints Do You Need?
To study your favorite design, one set of blueprints may be sufficient. On the other hand, if you plan to use contractors or subcontractors to complete the project, you will probably need more sets. Use the checklist below to estimate the number of sets you'll need.

_____ Owner
_____ Contractor or Subcontractor
_____ Building Materials Supplier
_____ Lender or Mortgage Source, if applicable
_____ Community Building Department for Permits
        (sometimes requires 2 sets)
_____ Subdivision Committee, if any
_____ Total Number of Sets

Blueprint Hotline
Call Toll Free 1-800-521-6797. We'll ship your order within two business days if you call us by 4:00 p.m. Eastern Time. When you order by phone, please be prepared to give us the Order Form Key Number shown in the box at the bottom of the Order Form.

By FAX: Copy the order form at right and send it on our FAX line: 1-800-224-6699 or 1-520-544-3086.

Canadian Customers
Order Toll-Free 1-800-561-4169
For faster service and plans that are modified for building in Canada, customers may now call in orders directly to our Canadian supplier of plans and charge the purchase to a charge card. Or, you may complete the order form at right, adding the current rate of exchange to all prices and mail in Canadian funds to:

        The Plan Centre
        60 Baffin Place
        Unit 5
        Waterloo, Ontario N2V 1Z7

By Fax Copy the Order Form at right and send it via our Canadian FAX line: 1-800-719-3291.

HOME PLANNERS, LLC,
Wholly owned by Hanley-Wood, Inc.
3275 WEST INA ROAD
SUITE 110, TUCSON, ARIZONA 85741

Please rush me the following :
_____ Set(s) of Custom Plan _____
     (See index and Price Schedule) $_____
_____ Additional identical blueprints in
     same order @ $10 per set. $_____
_____ Reverse blueprints @ $10 per set. $_____

POSTAGE AND HANDLING		
DELIVERY (Requires street address - No P.O. Boxes)		
• Regular Service (Allow 7-10 days delivery)	$15.00	$ _____
• Priority (Allow 4-5 days delivery)	$20.00	$ _____
• Express (Allow 3 days delivery)	$30.00	$ _____
CERTIFIED MAIL (Requires signature) If no street address available. (Allow 7-10 days delivery)	$20.00	$ _____
OVERSEAS DELIVERY Note: All delivery times are from date Blueprint Package is shipped.	Phone, FAX or Mail for Quote	

POSTAGE (From box above) $_____

SUB-TOTAL $_____

SALES TAX (AZ, MI, & WA residents, please add appropriate state and local sales tax.) $_____
TOTAL (Sub-total and tax) $_____

YOUR ADDRESS (please print)
Name_____
Street_____
City_____State_____Zip_____
Daytime telephone number (_____)_____

FOR CREDIT CARD ORDERS ONLY
Please fill in the information below:
Credit card number _____
Exp. Date: Month/Year _____
Check one ❑ Visa ❑ MasterCard ❑ Discover Card ❑ Amex
Signature _____

ORDER TOLL FREE
1-800-521-6797
OR 1-520-297-8200

Order Form Key
TB43

USEFUL FINISHING SOURCES

Architectural Antiques Exchange
715 N. Second St.
Philadelphia, PA 19123
(215) 922-3669
Fax (215) 922-3680
doors, entryways, fencing & gates, windows, mantels, bars, backbars, vintage plumbing

Anthony Wood Products, Inc.
P.O. Box 1081
Hillsboro, TX 76645
(817) 582-7225
FAX (817) 582-7620
arches, balusters, brackets, corbels, drops, finials, fretwork, gable trim, spindles, exterior porch parts

The Balmer Architectural Art Studios
9 Codeco Court
Don Mills, ONT M3A 1B6 Canada
(416) 449-2155
FAX (416) 449-3018
cartouches, centerpieces, festoons, finials, friezes, keystones, medallions, mouldings, pilasters, rosettes

Blue Ox Millworks
Foot of X St.
Eureka, CA 95501-0847
(800) 248-4259 (707) 444-3437
FAX (707) 444-0918
balusters, baseboards, doors & windows, gutters, mouldings, porches, posts, vergeboards, wainscoting

Cain Architectural Art Glass
Rt. 1 Box AAA
Bremo Bluff, VA 23022
(804) 842-3984
FAX (804) 842-1021
eveled glass, windows, custom beveling on traditional machinery

Classic Architectural Specialties
3223 Canton St.
Dallas, TX 75226
(214) 748-1668 (in Dallas)
(800) 662-1221
FAX (214) 748-7149
uncommon architectural features

Creative Openings
P.O. Box 4204
Bellingham, WA 98227
(360) 671-6420
FAX (360) 671-0207

Cumberland Woodcraft Co.
P.O. Drawer 609
Carlisle, PA 17013
(800) 367-1884 (outside of PA)
(717) 243-0063
FAX (717) 243-6502
balusters, brackets, carvings, corbels, doors, fretwork, mouldings, screen doors

Custom Ironwork, Inc.
P.O. Box 180
Union, KY 41091
(606) 384-4122
FAX (606) 384-4848
fencing & gates

Denninger Cupolas & Weathervanes
RD 1, Box 447
Middletown, NY 10940
(914) 343-2229 (Phone and Fax)
Internet site: www.denninger.com
cupolas, weather vanes, finials, caps

Elegant Entries
240 Washington St.
Auburn, MA 01501
(800) 343-3432 (508) 832-9898
FAX (508) 832-6874
beveled glass, doors, art glass

Focal Point Inc.
P.O. Box 93327
Atlanta, GA 30377-0327
(800) 662-5550 (404) 351-0820
FAX (404) 352-9049
arches, centerpieces, door & window casings, entryways, festoons, friezes, keystones, medallions, mouldings, rosettes

Gothom, Inc.
Box 421, 110 Main St.
Erin, ONT N0B 1T0 Canada
(519) 371-8345
FAX (519) 371-8268
balusters, porches, posts, screen doors, vergeboards

Mad River Woodworks Co.
Box 1067
Blue Lake, CA 95525-1067
(707) 668-5671
FAX (707) 668-5673
brackets, drops, entryways, finials, mouldings, posts, spandrels, wainscoting, siding, shingles

W.F. Norman Corporation
P.O. Box 323, 214 N. Cedar
Nevada, MO 64772-0323
(800) 641-4038 (417) 667-5552
FAX (417) 667-2708
balusters, brackets, cartouches, finials, friezes, keystones, mouldings, tin ceilings, metal roofs, siding

The Old Wagon Factory
P.O. Box 1427, Dept. PHE91
Clarksville, VA 23927
(804) 374-5787
FAX (804) 374-4646
storm screens

Ornamental Mouldings Limited
P.O. Box 336
Waterloo, ONT N2J 4A4 Canada
(519) 884-4080
FAX (519) 884-9692
in the United States:
P.O. Box 4068
Archdale, NC 27263-4068
baseboards, door & window casings, mouldings

The Renovators Supply
P.O. Box 2515
Conway, NH 03818
(800) 659-2211
FAX (603) 447-1717
classic hardware, plumbing, lighting and home decorating items

San Francisco Victoriana, Inc.
2070 Newcomb Ave.
San Francisco, CA 94124
(415) 648-0313
FAX (415) 648-2812
baseboards, brackets, centerpieces, door & window casings, festoons, medallions, mouldings, pilasters, posts, rosettes, wainscoting

The Millworks Inc.
P.O. Box 2987 - HPI
Durango, CO 81302
(800) 933-3930 (970) 259-5915
FAX (970) 259-5919
arches, balusters, baseboards, brackets, carvings, door and window casings, drops, keystones, mouldings, pilasters, porches, posts, screen doors, vergeboards, wainscoting, windows

Tennessee Fabricating co.
2025 York Ave.
Memphis, TN 38104
(901) 725-1548
FAX (901) 725-5954
brackets, fencing & gates, finials, porches

Vintage Wood Works
Highway 34
P.O. Box R
Quinlan, TX 75474
(903) 356-2158
FAX (903) 356-3023
arches, balusters, brackets, corbels, drops, finials, fretwork, gable decorations, porches, posts, spandrels, vergeboards